MINORU TAKEYAMA

Architectural Monographs No 42

MINORU TAKEYAMA

EDITED BY BOTOND BOGNAR

A.D. ACADEMY EDITIONS

ACKNOWLEDGEMENTS

All visual material and text is courtesy of the architect. Illustration of the Iwakura Residence on p46 shows furniture designed by H Klint and sculpture by S Tanaka.

Front Cover: Atrium, Mikakuto Office Tower, Osaka;
Frontispiece: Tokyo Port Terminal

Photographic credits:
Botond Bognar, pp8, 10 (U-House, Fantasy Villa), 12, 14, 16, 18, 20 (Nakamura Hospital, Renaissance Building), 32, 71, 72, 74/5, 79 (above left), 106, 107, 110, 112 (below); Courtesy of Nakamura Hospital p79; Mitsumasa Fujitsuka, pp34, 36 (below), 42, 46, 49, 50, 52, 53, 56 (above & below right), 58/9, 60, 62/3, 64 (below), 65 (above), 68 (above left), 69 (above right), (below left), 90, 91 (above); K Furudate, pp front cover, frontispiece, 6, 69 (model of cube), 76, 78, 80, 82, 83, 84, 86 (centre, below left & below right), 96 (above & below left), 97 (above right), 98, 100, 102, 103, 104, 108/9, 111, 112 (above right); Mishima, pp79 (below), 88, 97 (above left), 112 (above left); Tomio Ohashi, pp 40/1 (below),41 (above left); Shinkenchiku-sha, pp 35, 54, 66, 69, 91 (below left), 92/3,94; Masao Arai, pp40 (above right), 41 (above right), 48 (above), 57; Minoru Takeyama, pp20 (Mikakuto Sweet Factory), 24, 26, 44, 45

Architectural Monographs No. 42

First published in Great Britain in 1995 by
ACADEMY EDITIONS

An imprint of
ACADEMY GROUP LTD
42 Leinster Gardens London W2 3AN
Member of the VCH Publishing Group

ISBN 1 85490 281 4

Distributed to the trade in the United States of America by
ST MARTIN'S PRESS 175 Fifth Avenue, New York, NY 10010

Printed and bound in Singapore

CONTENTS

Takeyama – Heteropolitan
Charles Jencks   6

Reconciling Polar Opposites The Urban Architecture of Minoru Takeyama
Botond Bognar   8

Source of Meaning Diachrony of Intentions and its Background
Minoru Takeyama   22

PROJECTS

Takeyama – Heteropolitan

Introduction

by *Charles Jencks*

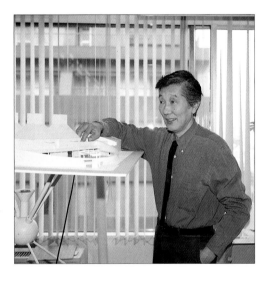

Minoru Takeyama

The architecture of Minoru Takeyama is much more versatile than that of the usual practitioner. Like his character, it is swift, elegant, changeable, humorous, moody and calm – even monumental. Impossible to classify in any style or school, apart from the pluralism of Post-Modernism, it is suited to the particular client and site without being a predictable contextual solution. For the bar area of Shinjuku, his famous Niban-kan took in the commercial Pop vernacular of the area and augmented its frenzied cacophony into a strong image – considered Post-Modern in 1975 (because of its hybrid Modern and commercial mixture). Today it would be seen as Deconstructionist. The labels don't matter particularly, although they highlight different aspects of his message, because it is the intensity and appropriateness of the architecture that counts.

For his Pepsi-Cola Bottling Factory in Mikasa and Hotel Beverly Tom in Hokkaido, Takeyama produced two amplified Neo-Classical buildings in a filigree, High-Tech style. Both structures conveyed their organisation, meaning and use through the outline form and in this way, could be considered heirs to *architecture parlante*, the semiotic architecture of Ledoux, Boullée, Lequeu and others at the end of the eighteenth century. Takeyama studied semiotics and has always been deeply involved with the way architecture communicates – both on the street and to different types of people, to those with different tastes and world views. Hence there exists a certain irony, ambiguity and double-meaning in all his work, and a willingness to incorporate heterogeneous materials, opposite sensibilities – the transient, kitsch and commercial as well as the monumental, serious and abstract.

For the Nakamura Memorial Hospital in Sapporo he has adopted a chaste, white Post-Modern Classical mode, turning the health facility into a large public monument that dominates a small part of the city. Purification, sterility, control and holistic balance are immediately conveyed through the spaces and harmonious forms. How different this is from his High-density Low-rise Housing Project of 1973, an *ad hoc* collection of small-scale forms and spaces played for its intricate domesticity, or – the most extraordinary domestic solution – his parents' house wrapped in a cocoon of metal sheathing to protect it from the noxious fumes, noise and terror of a busy Sapporo street.

I picture Takeyama, as I have often seen him as we walk the streets of Tokyo looking at new buildings and the carnival of the city. He is dressed in a dark acid-green corduroy suit – the American architect's garb of the 1960s, reflecting his Harvard training; he does look somewhat western, with a happy-sad grin, a Japanese Humphrey Bogart. Like others from the East who have trained and worked in the States, his thought and mannerisms are hybrid, accepting, gently ironic and in his case loaded with wry insights. His sardonic smile in the direction of an incongruous building – like a Bogart gesture – is comment enough. He does not seek to summarise the scene with a theory of urbanism or architecture, not for him the tidy systems of Le Corbusier, Darwin or the Metabolists. He does not sweep up messy reality into some overwhelming unity, or stylistic synthesis, nor suppress unwelcome facts like the Minimalist or perfectionist. In this inclusive, ironic pluralism and with an hybrid eastern-western personality, he is the quintessential Japanese Post-Modernist – even more than Kurokawa and Isozaki.

We stop by the side of an office building, where his atelier is crammed into several rooms, and survey the 'pencil buildings' that dot Tokyo. Across the street is a fashionable Miyawaki dress shop, so Minimalist-concrete that Pawson would eat his heart out wondering if he could get this much 'less'. The sidewalk is cramped; workers are jack-hammering the street to lay cables; cars push us onto the curb and then a wedding-procession in kimono and silk pushes us off. Just as we go into his office I see, shoved tight against the pencil, a perfectly traditional Shinto shrine. What the . . . ? Unbelievable – a fifteen foot temple which some neighbourhood group wouldn't sacrifice to the Tokyo boom. That just about summarises the whole beautiful mess that is Tokyo: rooftop golf, simulated sex, and second-century shrines crammed together with such intensity that Koolhaas' epitome of 'the culture of congestion' – New York City – looks like the open prairie, *lebensraum*, Antarctica. The signs of the street are riotous, conflicting, life-enhancing, horrible. Takeyama breaks into that tired, ironic, I've-seen-it-all-Bogart grin. He, as I, knows the lessons of Jane Jacobs because we were at Harvard at the same time understanding their challenge to Le Corbusier, his teacher Sert and the Modern paradigm.

Takeyama's response to the Jacobite-Corbusian collision is, naturally, to combine insights from enemy camps, to accept conflicting discourses, as might any good Buddhist. His non-theory is 'heterology in architecture', an enigmatic desire to 'confirm the relation between heterogeneous expression and homogeneous content'.(The riotous street life we see is anything but homogeneous in content, but perhaps he is referring to the way so much Machine Age life *does* reproduce identical demands, so many repeated units of this and that, identical urban tissue by the yard?)

His Tokyo International Port Terminal has this characteristic duality, and appropriately so since its function is the equivalent of an airport terminal by the sea, a place where foreigners arrive to find a new home and families break up to seek their fortune. A Constructivist, Corbusian or Late-Modern grammar (it's all three and none of them) is used to send partly traditional meanings – of welcome and departure, of landmark and ocean-liner, of city grid and *belvedere*. The idea of little house at the top, a conceptual *aedicule*, is represented by a steel-frame pyramid open to the sky. This ghost building – a typical flamboyant sign that Takeyama will use in his commercial buildings – is displaced from tradition and cliché because of the material. The metal-ghost also recalls the outline-buildings of Stirling and Venturi a decade earlier, but Takeyama does not care if he is ten years out of fashion since his hetero-architecture is so mixed as to be, in some respects, ten years ahead. Besides, like Bogart he's seen it all, knows all the arguments, has seen through them all and returned to them for inspiration: heteronomy, heteropolis, heterogeneity, heterosexuality, heterarchy, heterotopia, hetero-architecture.

His Post-Modern Classicism is every bit as inclusive as Robert Venturi's and he will actually use it on the commercial and industrial buildings that most High-Art architects would spurn. Because he takes on building commissions beyond the pale – Niban-kan has fourteen bars – because he is hard to classify, because he is from the northern province of Hokkaido, because he is subtle, changeable, poetic and perhaps more western than most Japanese – because of all these things, he hasn't found the acceptance that has gone to the established creators of Tokyo architecture – Tange, Isozaki, Kurokawa, Maki, Ando – and has remained something of an outsider. His contribution to Japanese architecture is no less important for that. Think of marginalised figures in American architecture such as Maybeck, Gill, Schindler, Sullivan and Wright – all more important to architecture than those who occupy the political centre, such as Skidmore Owings and Merrill. Takeyama is one of the few maverick poets who make the Japanese scene so vital, and different from the professional stereotype. He is Baudelaire's ideal Modernist, turning transient street-life into eternal formula, or the archetypal Post-Modernist operating in the gap between carnival and culture.

Reconciling Polar Opposites

The Urban Architecture of Minoru Takeyama

by *Botond Bognar*

Given that meaning is often split into opposite poles, for me the most trustworthy method of articulating (architecture) is to try to hold the opposing meanings in equilibrium . . . If we . . . architects, can discern and express meaningful opposites in the confusion of the urban environment, we may hope that the public could establish the semantic orientation of their own and that communication between the built environment and its users will be re-established.

To see [or perceive] things is already the beginning of creation.

Minoru Takeyama [1]

Shibuya Station Square, Tokyo, looking west towards the Tokyu 109 Building (1978), Minoru Takeyama

Most Western readers would remember Takeyama as the architect whose design, the Niban-kan Building, 1970, in Tokyo, was featured on the frontispiece of Charles Jencks' 1977 edition, and now classic book, *The Language of Post-Modern Architecture*.[2] It is therefore no surprise that Takeyama has ever since been considered an important representative of Post-Modernism not only in Japan, but perhaps also beyond. This position on the increasingly complex map of global architectural developments is indeed the most appropriate, and it still remains the cornerstone of delineating the significance of his work today. Yet, the general understanding of Takeyama as simply a Post-Modern designer, does not seem to give full justice to his multifaceted architecture, neither in terms of the specific buildings, nor in light of his, since then, much expanded overall output. This is so on the one hand, in as much as Post-Modern has by now become one of the most overused generic terms that means as many different things to as many people who use it; on the other hand, one is immediately reminded of the fact that Post-Modernism in Japan, more than anywhere else, burst on to the architectural scene with a dazzling diversity that shared only as much in common with one another as merely their mutual rejection of, and often joint origin in the tenets of Modernism itself. Takeyama's architecture therefore, now requires further examination and a more in-depth introduction.

Takeyama in Context

The work of Minoru Takeyama, one of Japan's leading architects in the past two and a half decades, can be summed up as complex and heterogeneous; he combines, even within individual projects, a wide variety of intentions and elements, often with contradictory meanings, in response to the paradoxical conditions that not only shape the urban and cultural landscape in Japan, but also inescapably, set the stage for his projects. 'The resultant hybrid[s], like all inclusive architecture,' as Jencks himself observed, 'balances and reconciles opposed meanings . . . [It] absorbs conflicting codes in an attempt to create "the difficult whole".'[3]

More precisely, Takeyama's designs can be characterised as being both populist and conceptual or, such as those which are equally endowed with the capacity for a 'common-sensical' or everyday communication, they possess an abstract quality that simultaneously challenges the very means of effortless disclosure and associations, or any communicative immediacy. In other words, his buildings, which exploit both the constructional or material aspects, and the semantic potential or *sign* character of architecture, are capable of 'speaking' in various voices while engaging their physical and social environment in both an affirmative and *critical* manner. In so doing, however, Takeyama's multivalent designs, remarkably, show almost no signs of the sentimental or the trivial. In fact, his recent works, with particular regard to the spectacular Tokyo International Port Terminal (1991), reveal an increased sensibility towards, and skill in utilising the powerful effects of both natural phenomena and latest media technology.

Educated both at Waseda University in Tokyo and Harvard University in the United States, and having worked several years in the USA and Denmark before establishing his own design office in Tokyo in 1965, and then a branch office in Sapporo in 1975, Takeyama is one of those few Japanese architects who, with substantial experience abroad, are able to combine Western and Japanese modes, or rather, languages of design in the most convincing way. To all these 'dual' qualifications it is necessary to add that, beyond being a highly successful practitioner, he is also an academician, who has a long-standing and distinguished teaching career at various universities, and whose theoretical work in the field of architectural and urban semiology is much recognised. In this regard Peter Popham remarked that 'Minoru Takeyama is almost alone among Japanese architects in being both academically respectable and street smart.'[4]

This too underscores the fact that Takeyama is not merely or simply an architect – at least not in the sense the profession is generally understood – but inseparably and very importantly, also an urbanist whose concerns in design address the city as much as, and often much more than, the specifics of architecture. For him, like many of his contemporaries, there are no rigid boundaries between a building and the urban realm; shaping the first is always equivalent to giving form and meaning to the second, while the second always 'sets the stage', that is to say, constitutes the context within which architecture can yield meanings of 'its own'. If this holds true in general, then it does even more so in Japan, where the city is more kaleidoscopic, disoriented, restless, and obtrusive than in other contemporary cultures; increasingly pervasive, the city in Japan is always at the doorstep of architecture as well as in the back of the architect's mind. Yet, the task of deciphering and responding to the paradoxical manifestations of the Japanese city is a formidable task, particularly if the designer wants to make sense within the process. And it is precisely the fostering of this complex give-and-take process, the reciprocal engagement between the city and architecture, wherein Takeyama's works have made the most substantial contribution to the cause of both Japanese architecture and urbanism; in their unusually difficult, polymorphous and polysemous context, they make sense in a curious way.

Takeyama's début with his first designs in the late 1960s, was not a moment too late to catch the swell of 'A New Wave of Japanese Architecture.'[5] In fact he was not merely riding with the surge, but was among the very first on the crest of it. In other words, he became one of the leaders of an emerging new generation of avant-garde architects whose aim was to instigate a refreshingly new spirit in architecture, a change which was also overdue in Japan. By this time Japanese Modernism, like the Modern movement worldwide, became stagnant, seemed exhausted, and, along with the utopias of Japanese Metabolism, both in terms of architecture and urbanism, was effectively overrun by the harsh realities of an unchecked industrialisation: congestion, pollution, etc, on the one hand, as well as by the effects of a rapidly progressing wholesale commercialism, on the other.

However the task here is not the forwarding of yet another assault on the inadequacies of Modernism, and this is particularly so, because, despite many of its justly criticised shortcomings, 'Modernity,' as Jurgen Habermas, and many others pointed out correctly, was left as 'An Incomplete Project', and as such, still capable of boasting untapped resources and a capacity for innovation.[6] As if to prove the point, this most important movement of the twentieth century, today shows powerful signs of comeback in architecture, but now – without its previous claim for universality and the consequent anonymity – in a re-energised and much enriched form. But the fact remains that the early 1970s marked a genuine disillusionment with the mechanising tendencies of International Modernism and its late Japanese counterpart, Metabolist architecture, which was too often obsessed with the application of industrial technology. Following the general tendencies, prompted not least by the worldwide energy crisis and recession, there emerged a significant shift in the attitudes of Japanese architects. The development of a new architectural thinking, coupled with new strategies in design, was not only necessary but also inevitable.

The New Wave and the Japanese City

These strategies were to evolve around the issue of architectural meaning. Modernist and Metabolist architects were preoccupied primarily with the elaboration and *consistency* of large, all-encompassing systems; strict master plans, dominant infrastructures and/or megastructures, but both apparently at the expense of the significance of everyday human experience. Seeing the futility and eventual failure of such persistently and *singularly idealistic* endeavours, representatives of the New Wave began to approach urban problems in a different way; they were determined to find meaning in the disposition and quality of the concrete elements in the immediate environment or, in *the city as is*; they were more inclined to look at architecture and urbanism from the multiple, but more realistic, 'down-to-earth' vantage-points of ordinary citizens and not merely 'from above' as Modernist designers did. The search for, and understanding of the existing *context* became of primary significance. As a result, the growing number of designs by this new generation of architects, trying to address the exceedingly multivalent Japanese built environment, turned out to be both much more *inclusive*, and widely divergent in their

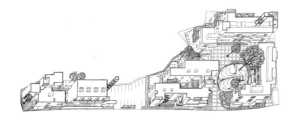

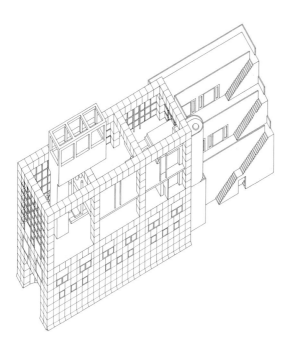

FROM ABOVE: *Hillside Terrace Apartments, Tokyo (1969-76), Fumihiko Maki; U-House in Nakano, Tokyo (1976), Toyo Ito; Fantasy Villa, Omi (1975), Osamu Ishiyama; Shukosha Building, Fukoka (1975), Arata Isozaki*

interpretations of architecture than the rather *exclusivist*, and often look-alike, 'purist' works of their predecessors.

In this regard, however, it is important to point out some apparent differences that existed between the developments of Japanese and other Western branches of Post-Modernism from the beginning. The new directions on the global stage of architecture, with special regard to the USA and even Europe, manifested, more often than not, a rather uncritical return to various historic precedents, a retreat to the comfort and 'safety' of the past. The works of Charles Moore, Michael Graves, not to mention Robert Stern, come to mind first as the best, but by no means only examples of this reactionary trend. Such explicit recycling of a formal history, just as much as the more implicit and more sophisticated *typological* operations of Aldo Rossi with European models of urban architecture, on the other hand, is largely missing from the oeuvre of the new generation architects in Japan, and for good reasons.

Japanese architecture, after its brief periods of flirting with the international style in both pre-war and post-war years, was to gradually and rather consistently explore various modes of integrating aspects of its traditions.[7] Through the pioneering works of Kenzo Tange, then later, Kunio Maekawa, Junzo Sakakura, and others, aesthetic, structural, and spatial characteristics of the post-and-beam wooden architecture were incorporated in new, reinforced concrete buildings, yet in ways that, by and large, bypassed reverting to the literal use of formal elements from the past. More interestingly, even the technologically inspired Metabolists, including Kiyonori Kikutake and Kisho Kurokawa, strived for, and often achieved, a high level synthesis between the rational demands of contemporary industrialised, Modern architecture, and the perceptive sensibilities of traditional design.

In other words, much more than the visible, it was the 'invisible', that provided continuity in the 'discontinuous' stages of Japanese architecture. One of the designers who greatly exemplified this ongoing process in Japan, was the ex-Metabolist Fumihiko Maki, whose work – unfolding in the late 1960s and early 1970s – was also a poignant demonstration of the important differences existing between a Japanese *contextualism* and its more formalistic counterparts in both the USA and Europe. In both his theoretical work, including the *Investigations in Collective Form* of 1964, and growing number of completed projects, such as the Hillside Terrace Apartment Complex in Tokyo (1969-1976), Maki outlined as well as successfully implemented a new understanding of architectural and urban design. Derivative of his idea of 'group-form', his designs became more responsive not only to 'the nature of the immediate environment . . . [but also] *the inner landscape of the collective consciousness of a culture*, which define . . . a context [of] architecture;' a distinctly Japanese approach indeed. [my italics][8]

As we shall see, Takeyama's approach, or what he called 'heterology', turned out to be another highly original and convincing mode of building upon the 'invisible' that connects various stages and phenomena of Japanese culture.

If a formal return to history was not a significant component of Japanese Post-Modernism, there were, surprisingly, many other design departures that did broaden the architectural spectrum of its vanguard, the New Wave. Issues, as well as problems surfacing in contemporary culture, society, and the city, filtered through the *individual* interpretations of the architects, provided ample incentives for various new design paradigms to evolve. Relieved from the restricting standards of Modernism, the new generation of Japanese designers was now free to explore as many directions as possible. These directions could be charted between two opposing interpretations of the urban conditions in Japan; at one end of the spectrum were the ones that manifested an explicitly negative attitude, or at best, remained neutral toward the city, and, at the other, the ones that responded to it in a more positive way.

Among the first one finds the works of Kazuo Shinohara and his 'school', Kazunari Sakamoto, Toyo Ito, Itsuko Hasegawa, and others, examining such abstract themes as 'absence', 'void', 'zero degree' while focusing on the qualities of *interior* spaces that often conjured up 'introspective utopias'; Hiroshi Hara's so called 'reflection houses' were both ritualistic and phenomenalistic in conception, but equally *introverted* in articulation. The spiritual or 'religious' dimension of architecture, and particularly the house, was frequently the subject of Kijo Rokkaku and Kiko Mozuna's designs, the latter extending it to mythological and even cosmic dimensions. The non-contextual architecture of Hiromi Fujii, on the other hand, was derivative of his frigidly rational, *structuralist* or syntactical operations that could liken him to the American Peter Eisenman. Even more importantly, Tadao Ando emerged as the champion of a 'minimalist' and 'defensive architecture' that, while reintroducing the poetic as well as provocative aspects of 'nature', turned its back on the city, thereby protecting the inhabitants from both the physical and psychological intrusions of the outside world.

Other intentions were not so oppositional to the existing urban conditions. Beyond Maki's 'investigations in collective form' toward the elaboration of his contextual architecture, another ex-Metabolist, Kisho Kurokawa was forwarding the issue of 'intermediary space' to mediate between architecture and the city. Younger designers were even more radical in their attempt to engage the built fabric around; Kazuhiro Ishii experimented with an easygoing, and often humorous mode of design that was breaking and/or transforming the syntactical rules or the grammar within the language of Japanese urbanism as much as it relied on them for conveying new meanings in his architecture. Team Zoo was dedicated to yet another paradigm, the *vernacular* in architecture, that was long forgotten by the Modernists, and Metabolists alike.

Osamu Ishiyama, on the other hand, was convinced that the quantity and variety of surplus products in an industrial society could and should be effectively utilised in architecture, and developed a language that may be called the *parody* of industrial vernacular blended with the 'lyricism of the junk.'

Of course, there were also others who attempted to combine the positive or conciliatory and negative or critical attitudes towards the predisposition and specific qualities of the Japanese city. Although such intentions can be detected, with varying degrees and in various ways, also in many of the cases mentioned above, they were the most conspicuous in Arata Isozaki and Minoru Takeyama's architecture. Indeed, the works of these two architects, despite their obvious differences, reveal remarkable affinities, which is evidenced first of all by the fact that their designs, perhaps more than anybody else's, encompassed a wider range of issues combining within their scope the frequently contradictory attributes of structuralism, abstractionism, contextualism, populism, Op-art, traits of humour, irony, and many others. In short, their architecture spanned and incorporated most of the intentions that the works of the new generation designers seemed to address independently, 'one' at a time.

Moreover, not only were these two architects the best representatives of a radically *pluralistic* new architecture, but also they had been the first in Japan to embark on the road towards it, and along which their generation eventually followed. It is in this sense that Takeyama, together with Isozaki, can be regarded as one of the 'fathers' of the New Wave in Japan. While the vast majority of the multifarious new directions erupted on to the scene around the first part of the 1970s, proliferating rapidly thereafter, Isozaki and Takeyama, as early as 1969 and 1970, had already completed such innovative projects as the Oita Medical Hall in Oita City, plus the Ichiban-kan and Niban-kan Buildings in Tokyo respectively, which were then followed by numerous others in close succession. Even Kiko Mozuna's pioneering and provocative Anti-dwelling House in Kushiro was finished only in 1971, and let us not forget that in 1969 Metabolism was still the unquestionable paradigm in architecture with many of its major accomplishments, including the Osaka Expo' 1970 and Kurokawa's Nakagin Capsule Tower of 1972 in Tokyo, yet to come.

Early Work

It is no wonder then that at the time of their completion the Ichiban-kan and Niban-kan, with their new mode of design and response to the urban context, were both truly contrasting and refreshing additions to contemporary Japanese architecture. What is surprising however, is the fact that today they look just as invigorating and appropriate in their mode of both blending into and challenging the prevailing, rather trivial and kitsch environment of Kabuki-cho, Shinjuku's famed nightly entertainment district, as they did some

FROM ABOVE: *Nakagin Capsule Tower, Tokyo (1972),
Kisho Kurokawa; Ichiban-kan, Tokyo (1969), Minoru
Takeyama; Niban-kan, Tokyo (1970), Minoru Takeyama*

twenty-five years ago. In addition to incorporating a series of commercial sign boards and name plates into their designs, Takeyama conceived of the two structures – which accommodate a host of pubs, bars and night clubs – with uniquely shaped geometric forms and strikingly painted, colourful surfaces and supergraphics as facades, that both define and dissolve these forms. As if covered with Op-art paintings by Vasarely, the Ichiban-kan and Niban-kan can appeal equally well to both the popular and highly abstract or elitist tastes in architecture. In this regard Vladimir Kristic had this to say:

> The most provocative aspect of [Takeyama's] design is that it accepts the madness and the absurdity of the Japanese city as an undeniable reality in which its own condition, and eventual resolution is embedded . . . The . . . building[s are] built around [the] contradicting realities of [their] external and internal worlds . . . [The] abstractness and unintelligibility of the building[s'] form denote the architect's desire to resist committing himself to either of the realities by leaving his architecture to float as a dematerialised object (sign) whose meaning (reality) is not performed and can only be circumstantially inscribed.[9]

Moreover the Niban-kan, in agreement with the owner, has been periodically repainted with different geometric (as well as numerical and lettered) patterns over the years, lending the building a curiously changing appearance and a more explicitly *sign* character. Indeed, rendering the Ichiban-kan and Niban-kan so as to approximate the quality of signs, beyond naming or denoting them merely as Buildings No 1 and No 2, was directly related to the surface manipulation of their 'skin'.[10] Takeyama himself admitted this by referring to his intentions as 'The Reinstatement of the Film Membrane', which was prompted by his 'discovery of the independent meaning of the membrane as an extremely visible boundary between interior and exterior, and as a tangible object invisibly establishing relations with a perception of existence'.[11] He also recognised that 'the surface around the exterior periphery of . . . things along the street is a concentration of multivalent signification. It seems . . . that, in Japan, cultural phenomena are expressed in the surfaces of everything'.[12]

Takeyama's understanding of the *quality of surfaceness*, or the notion of the membrane as *the most important locus of signification in Japan*, is already well detectable in his Labor Union Hall for the Fuji Heavy Industries, of 1970. He confirms this in an article by saying: ' . . . our intention was to turn the building, figuratively speaking, inside out and to allow the ornamental function of the exterior *membrane* to play an active spatial role.' [my italics][13] This recognition and his intention are brought home with particular poignancy and wit in the 'redesigning' of his parents' house in Sapporo in 1971. This old, and frail, traditional wooden townhouse, or *machiya*, located at a busy intersection of a major urban thoroughfare, and thus subject to the hazards and intrusions of the traffic which had vastly increased throughout the years, needed some protection and privacy. The necessity to provide such protection while keeping the house intact, led to the solution of wrapping around the entire structure with a layer of thin, corrugated, and diagonally painted aluminium panels – a telling gesture or *sign* of architecture's withdrawal? Or was it a 'play' of hiding in a 'box' or behind a 'mask' in the face of the onslaught of the city? If so, the operation can be likened to Ando's defensive architecture, but between the two there remains an important difference. Ando's early rejection of the city was always an uncompromising, and serious act of resistance, even fight, as manifested in his hard-surfaced and introverted, reinforced concrete structures; Takeyama's on the other hand was a radically schizophrenic, yet ambiguous gesture, in that, his new enveloping membrane not only shielded from, but also engaged the urban environment with the coquettish appeal of a 'pop' facade. It did, and continues to mirror the contemporary city, but again, by way of dissimilation rather than similitude, and in this sense, the mode of design here was also foretelling something of Toyo Ito's more recent architecture of 'lightness,' 'collage and superficiality,' first introduced in his PMT Building in Nagoya in 1978.[14] Therefore, as Kristic has once more correctly pointed out;

> Takeyama is a pop architect only as far as he recognises the inevitability of the commercialised condition of the city and accepts working within it. However, his architecture escapes the triviality of the 'decorated shed' philosophy by being devoid of any representational and associative meaning. The abstractness of . . . form [in his designs] defuses [the] communicative immediacy of [a] billboard architecture through the inconclusive nature of its physical composition, accessible to understanding only [by way of] interactive interpretation.[15]

Such *interactive interpretation* is exemplified in many Takeyama projects, but is particularly explicit in his designs for the 'Shu Pub', a chain of shoe stores in Tokyo (1970-80), where the painted patterns on the shoe boxes on shelves, and, by extension, the interior of the shops along with the 'meaning' of their space, change every time merchandise is sold from or restocked on the shelves. Another, and urbanistically more important example of this mode of design is the Atelier Indigo, Takeyama's own branch office and studio in Sapporo, completed in 1976. But more about this building later; first we have to return to the earlier stages of Takeyama's career as it unfolded along his search for the possibility of architectural meaning in the complexity of urban setting of Japan.

ArchiteXt

Upon returning home from abroad in 1964 with his fresh experiences in the new directions of European Western urbanism, Takeyama began to investigate the urban semiology, that is the urban language of the Japanese city. His long continued studies, particularly of Tokyo, resulted in several books and essays throughout the years, as well as led to the early development of his design theories centred around the notion of 'heterology in architecture'.[16] Prompted by the considerable success and recognition he had achieved with the application of his innovative design approach already within his first completed projects, Takeyama 'teamed up' with four other designers of similar interest; he became a founding 'member' and the undeclared leader of the so called ArchiteXt group which he formed in 1971 with Takefumi Aida (*b*1937), Takamitsu Azuma (*b*1933), Mayumi Miyawaki (*b*1936), and Makoto Suzuki (*b*1935).[17]

ArchiteXt was one of the most unusual 'groups' among the several – such as Basara, Archibrain, Archizoom, Archigram and Superstudio that popped up around that time – yet turned out to be the one which characterised best the times to come. It was established when the five architects came together to hold an exhibition in Tokyo in 1971, and decided to simultaneously launch a journal, to be edited by Takeyama – both with the title of ArchiteXt. Yet, beyond this, the group had no manifesto or joint statement to make, and in fact it did not even have a common line of design either; decidedly, it aimed at quite the opposite. These five devoted individuals continued to maintain their independent offices and different lines of design, and in effect remained, as before, merely an informal gathering of friends. One might even say that as soon as the group was formed it was also dissolved, thereby performing not only a successful media stunt, but an ultimate act of parody and, not least, paradox. Takeyama himself summarised their philosophy as 'discontinuous continuity', a rather telling commentary indeed.[18]

Nevertheless, apart from their different approaches to design, what connected these young professionals together was their shared interest in the communicative potential of architecture, or architecture as language, denoted by the selected name of ArchiteXt. To put it in another way, while the issue of exploring systems of architectural signs and the process of signification in design, like an invisible thread, ran through the activities of the 'members', the 'messages' they intended to convey were rather diverse; they were determined to challenge the totalitarianism of the 'one and only way of looking at things'. Obviously, they were sharply critical of both Modernism and Metabolism, while also using elements of these architectural precedents.

The issues of a reductionist form of collage, modulation of light, and a sensitivity to tactile qualities were in the centre mainly of Suzuki's projects which appeared to be acts of utmost restraint or self-denial as well; Miyawaki forwarded his 'primary architecture', a line of design that relied heavily on simple geometric forms with new spatial qualities primarily in the interiors, and on primary colours, often 'supergraphics', throughout the buildings but

FROM ABOVE: *Azuma Residence, Tokyo (1967), Takamitsu Azuma; Hotel Beverly Tom, Tomakomai (1973), Minoru Takeyama; Noa Building, Tokyo (1974), Seiichi Shirai*

mostly on the exteriors. On the other hand, Azuma, along with an intention to bring about '*polyphony in architecture*', favoured at that time a minimalist and introverted architecture, that was as much provoked by the exceedingly tight and aggressive urban conditions around, as it itself displayed both provocative and defensive attitudes toward the city. In this regard at least, Azuma's approach, best exemplified by his small residential designs, and particularly by his own remarkable house in Tokyo from 1967, therefore can be regarded as a forerunner of Ando's architecture, that was to commence in earnest only about a decade later. Aida, one of the most productive and innovative designers in the group, broadened the spectrum with his own *architecture of the absurd*, whose irrational rationality, derivative of a uniquely interpreted Oriental metaphysics, could manifest itself in various disguises including the 'architecture of silence', 'disappearing architecture' or an 'architecture of concealment', and 'architecture as toy'. The blank expressions of his Annihilation House, Nirvana House, House-like-a-Die, and the PL Institute Kindergarten, all from 1972 and 1973, represented actual forms and signs of a mute language or 'negative speech', and a reversed communication.

It is appropriate to say that ArchiteXt was an excellent representative of the *pluralistic* directions of the New Wave in Japanese architecture, and Takeyama, who was determined to pursue further the elaboration and implementation of his 'Heterology in Architecture', could only buttress such observation. Defining heterology as a mode of signification in contrast to 'analogy' and 'homology', he wrote:

> Heterology is a conception that establishes . . . relationship between two entities in terms of metaphysical meaning. The continuity can be measured by finding dissimilar or 'unlike' elements. For example, any comparison between a turtle's head and a mushroom would reveal that they have nothing in common . . . However, to the Japanese these two phenomena are both phallic symbols . . . Through heterology we can trace the continuous relationship between factors that are linked neither at the level of structure nor at the level of content, but in terms of their extrinsic [symbolic] meaning within a particular culture . . .

It is indeed an invisible connection that generates 'discontinuous continuities'.[19]

The Cylinder and the Cube

Takeyama's 'heterology' included, as one might expect, all or more, and at the same time, perhaps none of the directions his fellow members in ArchiteXt followed, while itself becoming steadily more multifaceted. Even so, around the early 1970s, certain elements of his design vocabulary seemed to emerge as more active and conspicuous than others. One of them was geometry. Although an intricate form of geometry had been an essential constituent of his previous works as well, it was gradually assigned a more significant role than before. Similar to Isozaki's interest in design around the 1970s, Takeyama, in several of his consecutive projects, began to investigate the potential of Platonic solids – rectangular or cubic, and circular or cylindrical shapes – in the process of architectural *signification*. This, furthermore, was also quite unlike the way Modernist architects approached geometry; their primary preoccupation was with the formal composition of *space*, often merely as a physical entity, that is a 'container' or volume, rather than human experience.

The first of the two geometric figures, that were assigned the role of relating architecture to its larger context and of giving special meaning to it, was the circle. Takeyama explained:

> . . . a context in which human undertakings are subordinate to the providence of nature began to develop within my intentions. Techniques have been used to contribute to an expression of human opposition [to] nature. This expression is based on the belief that humanity is of central importance. I however, was impelled to try to dissolve mankind in nature. This image took the form (Gestalt) of the circle, which is a basic rhythm in natural providence . . . The circle was a hypothesis developed in my intentions apart from the city and in the world of nature, but I reoriented it and made [it] a sortie against the city. The result of this step was the introduction of a further counter-positional method into my intentions . . . This counter-positional method expanded into a series of oppositions – space versus place, monumental versus responsive, and rational versus irrational.[20]

Takeyama's intentions, which seem to be imbued as much with the 'post-humanist' underpinnings of structuralism as, interestingly enough, with Japanese Shinto and Zen Buddhist philosophies of nature and humanity – are illustrated by two major projects. The designs of both the Pepsi-Cola Bottling Plant (1972) in Mikasa and the Hotel Beverly Tom (1973) in Tomakomai are derivative of the circle, or rather, the cylinder, while displaying several oppositional, or dual qualities. The two share the feature of having one quarter segment removed, and so, their cylindrical forms broken and opened up. Moreover, both of them have been designed with an 'empty centre' as their central cores, occupied by void, outside spaces, thus leaving only the peripheral zones for human occupation. Apart from this reversed or 'negative' use of the circle, however, the articulation and symbolism of the two are basically different.

On one level, the mode of design in case of the tower-like hotel is actually rather similar to Maki's contextualism. Located at the edge of the industrial port and a residential area of Tomakomai City with mountains and forests in the background, one of the assignments of the building was to mediate between the two; the 'open' white plastered facade seems to embrace the group of residences across the road and, beyond it, the presence of nature, while the other side, wrapped in blackened, lightweight concrete panels, responds to the various industrial facilities of the busy port by acting as a defensive shield. Nevertheless, looking at the Hotel merely from its 'darker side', Takeyama's design displays the essential insignia of a bizarre architecture, bringing it in close company with the uncanny work of Seiichi Shirai, especially his Noa Building in Tokyo (1974). Another, equally important intention of Takeyama was to express the vitality and dynamism of the fast developing city by creating a phallic symbol, which the mushroom shape denotes for the Japanese.[21]

Yet, the open geodesic dome crowning the hotel, is articulated so as to be significant in other ways as well. The spherical shape, that is also analogous with the human skull, might have actually had some personal significance to Takeyama, who had to undergo a serious brain operation a few years earlier, in 1970. In addition, the space beneath the steel lattice work – a rooftop terrace and observation deck – is a place where architecture comes face to face with nature, evoking even the dimension of the cosmic. This latter is evidenced by the unique mode of electric lighting the frame whereby, in the evening, the covering structure appears as the starlit sky or a planetarium. The spectacular illumination at the same time lends the building a manifestly festive mood, a quality that is apparent in many other projects by Takeyama.

The application of such high-tech, or media technology, along with the incorporation of various dome structures, returns with increasing frequency and sophistication in subsequent designs, such as his entry to the Centre Pompidou competition in Paris, culminating in the recent, and highly acclaimed Port Terminal Building in Tokyo (1991). In these projects, the domes as much as the circular and cylindrical forms, although often rendered by way of the latest high technologies, help him make architecture more responsive to the changing phenomena of nature, while providing also a critical device that aims at the city. The exception to this observation might be the Tokyu '109' building in Shibuya, Tokyo (1978), where the slender but solid, aluminium-panel clad cylindrical volume at the corner of the sharply angular site poignantly echoes the numerous, similarly shaped structures of rooftop commercials or advertisements, and in so doing, despite its rather straightforward, and almost 'silent' architecture, engages the urban fabric in a positive way; it has by now become one of the most significant and memorable urban elements in the area.

On the other hand, such efforts of Takeyama, have not always brought about such convincing results as the above examples. One of them is actually the Pepsi-Cola Bottling Plant, where, despite the attractively articulated architecture, the signifying capacity of the selected form is diminished by the form's decided 'inappropriateness' to the Plant's function, as well as location in wide open agricultural fields. It is true that Takeyama intended to avoid the building looking like a factory, in which respect he succeeded; the funnel form of the roof is suggestive of a stadium

FROM ABOVE: *Pepsi-Cola Bottling Plant (1972), Minoru Takeyama; Atelier Indigo, Sapporo (1976), Minoru Takeyama; Toy Block House No 7, Tokyo (1983),Takefuma Aida*

or amphitheatre. In a rather unorthodox manner, however, Takeyama is the first to admit the limitations of his design by saying: 'It was at the point of the production of this building that the counter-positional method became increasingly cynical.'[22] Somewhat jokingly, he also quotes a friend of his, who happened to remark on the Pepsi Plant this way: 'an irrational space for a rational process to produce irrational products.'[23]

While the circle and circular geometry were used for their affiliation with the natural and the 'irrational', Takeyama's simultaneous devotion to rectangular geometry and the cube, was for their capacity to address the artificial and the abstract in actuality, and so, by extension, also the dimension of the city.

'If there is such a thing as signs and codes in abstract reality, the minimum form will probably be the geometric cube', he himself said, yet added that his actual intention with the cube in architectural signification was:

to lift this morpheme from the world of the signifier and transpose it to the world of the signified . . . [In the future] the city and architecture will move away from the realm of physics toward the realm of biology and then to human perceptual structures. A new communal relationship will develop between human beings and things. My cube is a transitional intention aimed toward this kind of ultimate condition. At present, this is commissioned to achieve a situation in which architecture is cut free from space and is destined to produce closer relations with time.[24]

Takeyama produced various experimental projects with the cube to elaborate and test his theories in the form of numerous drawings and models. However, only two built designs actually illustrate his intentions well: the Iwakura Residence in Tomakomai (1973) and his own studio, the Atelier Indigo in Sapporo (1976). The uniquely articulated residence was developed as a pilot project of, and is closely related to a large scale proposal for a High-density Low-rise Housing Project (1973) in Tomakomai City, Hokkaido. In this project Takeyama envisioned an elaborate system of staggered and interconnected linear conduits, whose concrete box-beam structure, elevated above ground on pilotis, served multiple purposes; housing some of the infrastructure inside – heating and air-conditioning pipes, electric cables – it also defined a system of 'corridors' underneath – for common circulation – while delineating individual lots and territories. Filling in-between areas with living spaces and courtyards, and connecting horizontally stretching lines of conduits with prefabricated, bridge-like spatial units of additional rooms, the scheme was to gradually unfold into the intricately dense matrix of a Japanese 'urban village', whose additive and user-variable elements possess significant flexibility within the more stable 'syntax' of the infrastructure.

One does not have to know too much about the architectural developments in Japan in the previous decade to realise Takeyama's project comes strikingly close to the numerous urban schemes that Metabolist architects forwarded in the 1960s and wherein the emphasis was on the flexibility and interchangeability of constituent elements within or upon an overall organising infra- and/or mega-structure. Yet, any such resemblance between the two is somewhat misleading. If this is true in the case of the High-density Low-rise Housing and the Iwakura Residence, then it is equally or, perhaps more so in the Atelier Indigo. Here the modular design of the storey-high substructure with simple geometric shapes is complemented on the rooftop by a unique, cubical element, that in itself is comprised of eight smaller cubes and their sixteen, smaller parts. This rooftop element, used for various outdoor activities, exhibitions and shows is an 'infinitely' variable device, what Takeyama called 'a space synthesizer performing in an *ad hoc* fashion the constantly altering combinations of architectural language.'[25]

Thus, the apparently Metabolist design also reveals the architect's true intentions: the manually operable, low-tech mechanism, rather than trying to forward and better the principles of Metabolist architecture, seems to merely mock them, but in so doing, also rely on them. In effect, Takeyama's design was meant to be a sign of the passing time; the expression of time in relation to the spaces which are regularly altered and recreated by the users. Thus the large cube becomes a curious clock that imprints space, or rather, time in the life of the building and its architecture. In Takeyama's words:

> Alterations . . . (of the cubes over the Atelier Indigo) are unrelated to aesthetics and are free of substantial space-orchestration, because they are in themselves an expansion of *signification*. They have become different signs, resembling the hands of a clock. [my italics][26]

On the other hand, Takeyama's device, something like a giant 'Rubik's Cube', or a set of huge toy-blocks, does not lack the dimension and quality of an architectural toy either. In this regard one is immediately reminded of Takefumi Aida's so called 'toy-block houses', a series of ten projects that he produced in the late 1970s and early 1980s, and where the compositional units (vocabulary) were also the simplest geometrical solids. Yet, any comparison between the two architectures would have to point out a major difference; while Takeyama's blocks comprised a kinetic, and so an effectively generative or (inter)active, as well as abstract system, Aida's were adding up to more *passive* and populist compositions, the static *signs* of often painted block-like units or 'doll houses'. While these toy-blocks guided the design process in a way similar to the techniques of typology in Aldo Rossi's 'analogous architecture', Aida's *modus operandi* was much less rational with a result never really ascetic.

Work in the 1980s

The 1980s indicated a gradual shift in Takeyama's work. Semiological operations continued to play a significant role in his architecture, although were often kept in check by more 'pragmatic' requirements and considerations, and so, were perhaps less pronounced than before. On the other hand, one can observe the emergence of a new type of symbolic space that was to enrich his more recent designs with the dimension of the *phenomenal*. The Nakamura Memorial Hospital (1980), the neuro-surgical centre in Sapporo, is imbued with implicit references and a subtle symbolism of the human body, with particular regard to the brain and skull, that is the head; notice for example the extensive round shapes of the roof lines of the meticulously symmetrical building.

Admittedly, Takeyama's vision here, beyond trying to synthesise the attributes of Western and Eastern medicine, was to make the design inside, as much as possible, analogous to the image of the sitting Yakushi Nyorai, the Buddha of Healing. Accordingly, every department in the hospital would be at the place where the relevant part or organ of the body is located – a truly fascinating idea indeed. Yet, since there are clearly serious limitations to the extent within which such a scheme can be effectively realised, it is difficult to imagine that patients or visitors could see such an analogy in the building, without knowing about the designer's intentions. Nonetheless, the well balanced, crisply articulated, and pristine architecture that has been realised, is confidence inspiring, and reassuring for visitors and patients alike making it both an attractive health care facility and an important landmark in its urban setting.

The result, in terms of the intended signification, is somewhat similar in many ways to that within the innovative designs of Takeyama's Building No 10 of the Musashino Art Institute (1981), and the Mikakuto 'Sweet' Factory (1984), where the respective goals were to shape the long skylights over an internal atrium in the form of the Chinese character denoting 'beauty', while trying to wrap the industrial facility in 'sugar-coating' in order to both express the nature of the building's internal activity, and, at the same time, also hide it behind the lively and colourful, painted surfaces of its layered front walls. Between the road and these walls, which, fortunately, despite their 'coating', have nothing to do with any literally, or syrupy representation of a 'sweet' factory, Takeyama designed a 'fairy tale park' that, with its numerous small and playful sculptures, like chocolate figurines, is also an appropriate and inviting place for both children and grown-ups.

In regard to the difficulty of working in an historically significant environment, one should also mention another important Takeyama building, the Kyoto Renaissance (1986), which is situated at the east end of the station plaza, at the gateway to this ancient capital of Japan. The seven-storey building displays many outstanding qualities, not least the designer's intention to mediate between the

ABOVE: *Sapporo Factory, Sapporo (1993), Minoru Takeyama (design co-ordinator)*; BELOW: *Tokyo International Port Terminal (1991) at night, Minoru Takeyama*

city's historic atmosphere – imparted by hundreds of the most famous and revered Buddhist Temples with their gardens, and innumerable Shinto Shrines – and the newly acquired disposition as a centre for high technology research and industry. The applied details, materials, colour scheme, and, more importantly, the well selected motives or signs as references to the dual qualities of the setting, seem to give ample reason for the design to be successful. Yet, it is only partially so; due mainly to very restrictive regulations in the city, and extensive programmatic requirements, the Renaissance is less convincing urbanistically, than it could have been. It does not seem to match the witty poignancy of many of its predecessors in Takeyama's work. About the building Peter Popham commented this way:

> In some ways Renaissance rebuffs and rebukes Kyoto; in other ways it pays the city secret homage. It eloquently suggests how magnificently modern Kyoto might be – but does not care to take its own proposal too seriously. Like [Isozaki's] Tsukuba Center Building it is perhaps too complex and unhappy to be wholly satisfactory; but it offers a fascinating challenge and precedent to any other serious architect who might be tempted to build in Kyoto's heart.[27]

The review of Takeyama's architecture of the 1980s reveals that, while his pursuit of signification by emblematic forms and motives continued with varying intensity and somewhat uneven success, his professionalism attained a higher, more refined level. The latter is manifested in his mastery of details, materials – as seen in such projects as the Nakamura Hospital, Renaissance, the Egyptian Embassy, the five Office Towers – and, not least, it is also evidenced in the more frequent appearance of a *phenomenal* space, whose 'reading' and significance could only be deciphered phenomenologically or, by setting into motion an even wider range of human sensibilities than before. Such spaces are invariably built upon the intangible and the profoundly poetic in architecture, that encompass the changing and unpredictable manifestations of both nature and human artifice, including the city, altogether conjuring up the cosmic and the *metaphysical* in human experience.

Early forms of a phenomenal space appeared already in the Pepsi-Cola Bottling Plant, and more so, in the Hotel Beverly Tom, under the geodesic dome on the roof; it continued in the central atrium space of the Musashino Art Institute Building No 10 and the Mikakuto Sweet Factory, where the light, transparent roof between the old and new buildings define an elusive space of sparkling light and animated shadows. Even more poignant is the multi-storey atrium in the Nakamura Hospital that connects the higher block with the lower one, and wherein, according to Takeyama's anthropomorphic scheme, it could symbolise the sacred, innermost part of the building; reflective and light in colour, washed in the changing spectrum of light cascading down through the large, vaulted glass roof, this evanescent and captivating space is truly suggestive of the heart and soul of architecture. Other examples showing the evolution of a new space include such large-scale complexes as the Sapporo Factory (1993) and the Terme Hotel (1992), where, a large, urban scale atrium provides an active public place, once more blurring the boundary between architecture and the city. The symbolic space reappears also in the memorial hall of the Yokohama North Crematorium project, scheduled to be completed in 1999.

This new, 'phenomenal space' is undoubtedly the locus of information exchange, a point of various intersecting 'languages' and messages; it is thus another opportunity for signification, another realm for bringing together all the many, all too often, opposing forces, styles, sentiments, and meanings that shape both the physical environment, the city, and the range of human experience, individual as well as social. Takeyama's recent Tokyo International Port Terminal is the most powerful and poetic testimony to his success in pursuing a new phenomenal space and his heterology in architecture.

Reconciling Polar Opposites – Tokyo Port Terminal [28]

Located on the southeast corner of Harumi, a reclaimed island in Tokyo Port, the Terminal Building finds itself at the border of the city and the sea, or the man-made and the natural, between downtown and industrial areas and, obviously, it is also a point of both arrival and departure. Therefore Takeyama has shaped the complex so that, for those arriving by sea, the structure could signify a point of landing or 'landmark', while for those departing from land, it could also indicate the beginning of the sea and water; thus it is also a 'watermark'. On the one hand, the Terminal is articulated as a large house (or belvedere) on a hill, denoting arrival and home for those who are about to land; on the other hand, it may appear as a lighthouse by the sea for those coming from the city, and this latter quality is particularly evident when the building is lit in the evening. In addition, with its bridges, masts and sharply angled walls the overall scheme also suggests the image of an ocean liner.

The building is comprised of two basic parts: a widespread solid base structure with extensive sloping edges and, over this artificial 'hill', a more abstract, geometrically shaped, cage-like structure – the conceptual house – that envelopes a four-storey glass box with four interconnected tent domes on *and* under the roof. The base also features large rooftop terraces that are directly accessible from the street by way of wide stairways. These stairways and platforms – not unlike the ones in some recent projects by Ando – are prominent features of this part of the building. Circulation or movement however is also a primary force in shaping the upper part; a pair of elevator shafts, as independent towers, connect to the house-like structure and the observation decks on top, via bridges on two levels. They play a key role in the

FROM ABOVE: *Nakamura Memorial Hospital, Sapporo (1979), Minoru Takeyama, interior of atrium; Mikakuto Sweet Factory, Nara (1984), Minoru Takeyama; Renaissance Building, Kyoto (1986), Minoru Takeyama*

tectonics, and the dynamic structural expression of the building, in a way that seems to recollect the attributes of both Metabolist and Constructivist architecture.

In his attempt to address and resolve the issues of duality, Takeyama explored other possibilities as well; he has introduced two intersecting axes that organise the entire design. Elements along the perimeter of the Terminal complex, including the boarding platforms and most of the base, follow the rectangular geometry or street pattern of Harumi, and comprise the 'land' axis. Almost everything else, including the major outdoor stairways, and observation platforms, complies with the other directional locus. Set obliquely, in the direction of the new suspension bridge over the gateway to the port, this represents the 'sea' axis. The dynamic interaction between the two axial geometries heightens the building's already powerful formal disposition.

While all these considerations seemingly deal with only the physical conditions of the site, Takeyama's design goes beyond the immediately 'obvious' attributes of the location to address its 'hidden' dimensions or qualities of place. In so doing, the building acquires the qualities of the phenomenal, whereas the experience becomes unavoidably phenomenological. Accordingly, some of the most important aspects of the design are revealed through personal discovery. 'Naturally', many of these aspects relate to the changing and often unpredictable natural phenomena and human events: light-and-shadow effects; the sound and reflections of water; the sense of wind; movement of people; ships; that is, the life of the port and the city.

The numerous spectacles include such important elements as the lacy fabric of the enveloping steel lattice work that, while constituting a 'soft' or ambiguous boundary, lends phenomenal lightness to the upper part of the building. The visitors' experience however, culminates at the top, under the pyramidal open frame of the roof. This space, with several stepped observation platforms, is animated not only by the penetration of wind, but also by light; the four Teflon fibre 'domes', hit by the sun, appear to glow, and float like parachutes in the air. This effect of phenomenal lightness is doubled in the evening when the entire complex is lit and turned into another spectacular light show. Takeyama has thus managed to combine the benefits of both urban and natural phenomena in a convincing way and with their help, choreograph the project as an attractive and lively place at the edge of the city.

Equally representing the best attributes of popular and high art, while being derivative of contemporary high technology and construction, Takeyama's Port Terminal, summarising the best of his architecture, once again recognises, but not necessarily endorses the paradoxical and all too often absurd reality of the physical as well as semantic environment of the Japanese city. In other words, the 'building ... maintains a curious capacity by which it is able to both exploit, yet also reject the volatile cacophony of the Megalopolis.'[29] Drawing from the most disparate sources, while aspiring to a diversity of goals, Takeyama's inclusive, yet never trivial architecture manages to establish a meaningful dialogue, and eventually attain a lasting consensus between the opposite qualities and forces delineated by the conditions of his respective works. In so doing, his designs, 'instead of radically reorganising, [or] redefining the existing city, make a minute but telling difference.'[30] And this is by no means an insignificant achievement in Japan today.

Footnotes

1 M Takeyama in *Minoru Takeyama: 1989-90 recipient of the Plym Distinguished Professorship in Architecture*, Champaign-Urbana School of Architecture (University of Illinois)1989, p9.

2 C Jencks, *The Language of Post-Modern Architecture*, Academy Editions (London) 1977.

3 Ibid p90.

4 P Popham, 'Building in Kyoto "The Beautiful",' *The Japan Architect* 87:01 January 1987, p28.

5 'A New Wave of Japanese Architecture' was a large-scale travelling exhibition and lecture series touring major cities in the United States in 1978. Both exhibition and accompanying catalogue, edited by Kenneth Frampton and published by IAUS, New York, 1978, were organised to introduce the work of the new avant-garde in Japanese architecture emerging in the 1970s.

6 J Habermas, 'Modernity – An Incomplete Project', in Hal Foster (ed), *The Anti-Aesthetic – Essays on Postmodern Culture*, Bay Press (Washington) 1983, p3.

7 The 'international style' was emerging in the practice of a few pre-war architects, such as Kunio Maekawa, Tetsuro Yoshida, etc, in the early 1930s before the reactionary political climate successfully suppressed such endeavours by the latter part of the decade. After the war, the new democratic society, along with the urgency of reconstruction and the scarcity of means, resurrected this style, which manifested itself again in several works of Maekawa, Kenzo Tange and others, until about the early 1950s.

8 F Maki, *Investigations in Collective Form*, A special publication No 3, The School of Architecture, Washington University (St.Louis, MO) 1964 F. Maki, 'Fumihiko Maki' in K. Frampton (ed), *A New Wave of Japanese Architecture – Catalogue No.10*, IAUS (New York) 1978, pp74-5.

9 V Kristic, 'Minoru Takeyama: Ichiban-kan Multi-use building, Tokyo, 1968-70' in Colin Naylor (ed), *Contemporary Masterworks*, St. James Press (Chicago and London) 1991, p479.

10 The names of the buildings are also painted in large supergraphics on the facades of both the Ichiban-kan and Niban-kan.

11 M Takeyama, 'The Reinstatement of the Film Membrane', *JA*, 70:08 August 1970, p70.

12 M Takeyama, 'Heterology In Architecture', *JA*, Special Issue featuring ArchiteXt, 76:06 June 1976, p72.

13 M Takeyama, 'The Reinstatement of the Film Membrane', op cit 11

14 T Ito, 'Collage and Superficiality in Architecture', in K. Frampton (ed), *A New Wave of Japanese Architecture*, op cit 8 p68.

15 V Krstic, op cit 9.

16 M Takeyama, 'Heterology In Architecture', op cit 12.

17 Ibid.

18 Ibid, p71

19 M Takeyama, 'Heterology in Architecture', in K. Frampton (ed), *A New Wave of Japanese Architecture*, op cit 8 p86.

20 M Takeyama, 'Heterology In Architecture', op cit 12 p75.

21 The phallic image is also a very important fertility symbol in Japan; there are numerous Shinto shrines dedicated to fertility, and its symbols are often displayed during numerous annual Shinto religious rituals and festivals.

22 M Takeyama, 'Heterology in Architecture', op cit 12 p75.

23 Ibid.

24 Ibid pp76-77.

25 M Takeyama, 'Atelier Indigo', *JA*, 78:01, January 1978, p21.

26 M Takeyama, 'Heterology in Architecture', op cit 12 p78.

27 P Popham, 'Building in Kyoto "The Beautiful",' op cit 4.

28 This part of the text on the Tokyo Port Terminal is largely based on B Bognar, 'Architecture at the Edge of the City – The New Tokyo Port Terminal Building', in *Shinkenchiku* , 08/1991, pp265-6 (in Japanese).

29 B Bognar, in *Minoru Takeyama: 1989-90 recipient of the Plym Distinguished Professorship In Architecture*, op cit 1 p10.

30 Ibid.

Source of Meaning

Diachrony of Intentions and Its Background

by *Minoru Takeyama*

Preliminary scheme for Building No 10, Musashino Art University

Relativity

If one accepts that one role of architects in society is to express meaning in their culture and to make sense of the environment, then how do they accomplish this in the very ambivalent world in which most of them now live? Currently, the waves of architecture follow each other in rapid succession only to break up and be reassimilated into other waves. Given such a fluid and rapidly changing situation, how do they find a valid basis or starting point from which to design?

In response to these questions, some architects have been searching for a pluralistic language incorporating every tradition and tendency in an effort to produce a genuinely multivalent architecture. But the results are only meaningful to insiders. For the public at large their works are mostly a 'salad of words' which attracts only neuro-pathologists' attention without any real cultural meaning or resonance.

While architecture may appear to have achieved a global syntax, the truth is that this syntax is filtered through a multitude of cultural screens that differ with each individual community. Subtle shifts of meaning occur from one place to the next. Unless one is attuned to this, it is all too easy to misread the signs. In this respect, many architects are like tourists, projecting their own values and biases on to particular cultures. What may appear acceptable or unacceptable to them as outsiders in a given setting may be altogether the reverse to its inhabitants.

Although I was born and educated in Japan, I also trained in the USA, living and working there and in Europe, returning only later to establish a practice in Tokyo and Sapporo. Looking back, I see that in the earlier stages my primary interest was to apply what I had learned from the outside to the particular situations that I found in my work in Japan. In time however, my interests changed, and I began to generalise about architecture and society based on what I learned from each case and circumstance. I recognised that so many of these particularities needed to be comprehended and evaluated in the general view.

I find that the particularity of my work often contains and embraces a relativity which has a more general meaning and value. I could fall back on the terms of logic to name this process, but the methods of architecture are more opportunistic and subversive than strictly logical. 'Abduction' is therefore an apt name for this process of understanding and responding to the particularity that we experience, with open and relatively objective eyes, allowing its meaning to enrich our world rather than imposing our world upon it. Otherwise I fear a univalence shall extend over the earth and the universal world will come again.

Homogeneity Vs Heterogeneity

My return to Tokyo in 1964, after being away for six years in the USA and Europe, was a surprising rediscovery. The city had transformed greatly with an immense variety of morphological effects jammed into the streets. It was the year the Olympic games were held in Tokyo. Besides the obvious economic impact, the event was a symbolic epoch for the nation's future growth. In fact, the 1964 Olympics transformed Tokyo in much the same way as the Great Kanto Earthquake in 1923 or the aftermath of the disasters of the Second World War. These three events, although their results were different, functioned as catalysts for the tremendous volume of construction and urban growth that followed.

At first glance, the city appeared to be like a huge kaleidoscope of signs and presented extremely heterogeneous visions. With a little effort however, I saw that, no matter how heterogeneous the surface, society's hidden dimensions were still ruled by homogeneity.

For instance, with the help of advanced technology, information was extremely diverse in terms of form and surface, yet surprisingly uniform in its content. At this time, Japan's post-war, recovery economy was transferring to one that exported far more than it imported. With information, however, the opposite was true: Japan has always been a 'net importer' of every type of media and imported much more than it exported. Statistics from a publishers' conference at that time found that Japan published about twelve times more material about the USA and England than those countries published about Japan. This phenomenon concerning cultural information seems even more radical today. The point however, is not the quantity, but the particular quality that people are interested in or generally value. The ruling tastes and trends of the Japanese remain surprisingly univalent.

The cultural homogeneity of this country has been the result of racial, ethnic, religious, and linguistic uniformity, as many scholars point out. My intuitive reaction to this phenomenon was to search for the relationship between the heterogeneous expression visible on the surface and the homogeneous content hidden below.

I believe that comprehending the relationship between expression and content is one of the major tasks for architects, and forms the basis of their creativity. My hypothesis, after exploring this relationship in Japan for thirty years, is that the homogeneity of its cultural content is manifested inversely in heterogeneous expression, or the heterogeneity of expression in Japanese architecture is inversely related to the cultural homogeneity which underlies it and forms its real content.

Brother or Neighbour
Learning from my Teaching Experiences

I had several opportunities to test this hypothesis in design studios while teaching at universities in Japan and America including the University of California, Berkeley, Harvard University and the University of Illinois at Urbana-Champaign. Several times, I gave American students a design problem similar in content to one I had given to my students in Tokyo. The students' reaction in these two countries confirmed my own observations, theories and intentions.

One of the problems given to UC Berkeley students was called 'Broadway 77' and was developed with Robert Herman and Jennifer Clements, two San Francisco architects who also taught at UC Berkeley. Broadway, where it passes through the North Beach neighbourhood, is the principal entertainment strip in San Francisco. We first asked students to study this street as a distinctive part of the urban fabric, and then express their understanding of its streetscape through a design for a particular site on that street. One of the reasons for selecting this part of Broadway was that its visually heterogeneous and chaotic context reminds me of some Tokyo streets, one of which, Omotesando, I had used for a similar problem for the students in my studio at Musashino Art University in Tokyo.

When faced with this problem, none of the Japanese students paid the slightest attention to the existing visual 'codes' of the street. Instead of designing something to fit in with Ometesando's existing environment, they produced buildings that, in many cases, they had never experienced in reality, particularly in the vicinity of that street. In fact some of the projects could not be entered by a normal circulation route. One needed a pair of wings to make an entry! Others were vigorous pieces of contemporary urban sculpture, devoid of any architectural syntax.

I anticipated a similar response from my American students, but found instead that, without exception, their schemes maintained the existing syntax and context of the Broadway streetscape. Building heights, silhouettes, skyline, scale and proportion of windows and doors, gables and ornamentation all tended to retain the prevailing physical character of the street. No matter how freely they articulated their individual statements, they also wanted to participate in the existing street and preserve a continuity they had recognised in the overall visual effect.

The different responses to this problem suggested to me that the Americans looked for and found a visual continuity in their streetscape. The Japanese on the other hand, neither looked for nor perceived continuity in the existing reality but imagined an unrealistic continuity, detached and discontinuous from physical reality. As urban phenomena, Broadway and Omotesando are similarly multivalent and heterogeneous. Yet they presented or transmitted substantially different meanings to my American and Japanese students.

The contrasting attitudes of the two groups of students from different cultural climates reveal basic differences in cultural perceptions of the urban environment with respect to understanding what gives it meaning. In them I see two different and contrasting patterns of reading the given context. Broadway is perceived by the American students as continuous in presence, or *syntagmatic*. Omotesando is seen by the Japanese students as being continuous in absence, or *paradigmatic*. To borrow Roland Barthes' statement,

Takeyama's parents' townhouse in Sapporo
transformed with aluminium panels

syntagm is 'reading the restaurant menu vertically', while paradigm is 'reading it horizontally'. The common objective of the American students was to find a 'new neighbour' for the existing neighbourhood. The Japanese students, however, were anxious to discover an unknown 'brother' yet to be born, for the sake of the future brotherhood.

In both cases, architectural creativity was viewed as an attempt to affirm some kind of continuity in a multivalent world, thereby broadening and deepening the meaning of architecture.

Heterology

When I use the terms 'homogeneity' and 'heterogeneity', in the simplest sense I am referring to qualities of likeness and unlikeness. We orient ourselves in the world, and confirm our existence in it, by establishing a continuity of meaning (likeness) between different things – people, objects, places, concepts. Modern architecture is in part about the desire to achieve a greater continuity in spatial organisation, free from 'artificial' restrictions.

In my hypothetical analysis, this desire developed through three different stages; *analogy*, *homology*, and *heterology*. At each stage the meaning of continuity changed and the polarity of 'likeness' and 'unlikeness' made different counterbalances.

In short, *analogy* associates similar contents in spite of different manifestations of form and structure. For a simple visual example, a bird's wing and an insect's wing are very much alike, but only in terms of functional content. *Homology* on the other hand, permits us to establish formal similarity without regarding content such as function. For example, to some analytical eyes informed about biological evolution, a bird's wing and a dog's foreleg are structurally and formally similar. They share the same evolutionary tree yet are functionally unrelated. In the cases of both *analogy* and *homology*, a continuity occurs between two substances because of similarity or 'likeness', in either expression or content.

Is there any continuity possible between two items which could be measured by 'dissimilarity' or 'unlikeness'? If so, it will only be read by, or accessible to a limited audience who share the same sub-culture. For example, any comparison between a turtle's head and a piece of mushroom would reveal their forms and biological content have nothing in common. However, for most Japanese these two things share the same symbolic meaning. They are phallic representations and are widely used in literature, arts and the daily rhetoric of this country. I use the word *heterology* to describe this 'discontinuous continuity' that occurs when relationships are found between unrelated substances or among diverse meanings. Symbolic language often falls into this category, as for example in the various signs of Jesus; the Lamb, the dove, the fish. In the context of Christianity, these biologically different things stand equally for Him.

Of the three, *heterology* alone addresses the possibility of establishing continuity between apparently dissimilar things. That is, it offers the possibility of 'likeness' in the face of 'unlikeness' – a discontinuous continuity, if you will, that links things that have a related meaning in a particular context. Heterology is a useful tool to cope with the increasing heterogeneity of our living environment.

In my observation, I have found that *heterology* is oriented toward the uncertainty of our evolving built environment. It has changed from rural to urban through successive stages of industrialisation and has been transformed by the impact of the Age of Information. With this the concepts of continuity have evolved as well, passing from the stage of analogy through homology to that of heterology.

Surface Meaning

Going back to my return to Tokyo in 1964, I was genuinely astonished by the city's booming construction activities surrounding the Olympic games. Tokyo is the most concentrated capital of any nation in the world, accommodating about a quarter of the country's population within its metropolitan area. Thus, the attention of the entire nation was focused on this major event taking place in the city.

My relocation to Tokyo under these circumstances was so dramatic that using intuitive evaluation was the only way to readjust to existence in this kaleidoscope of signs. I read the most meaningful activities on the surface of the urban landscape in order to decode the hidden dimension below. The surface gave me accurate, direct and virtual messages and seemed to function like it would on a unicellular organism. Contrary to its large-scale urban activities, the city looked like a huge amoeba.

In a unicellular organism, the cell is encapsulated in a membrane which functions as a communication link between inside life and external stimuli. The membrane, or surface of the organism is more meaningful to the outside than it is to what happens inside.

Just like the membrane of a primitive organism, the surface of the buildings along Tokyo's city streets conveyed messages that exposed the meaning of the whole city to the outside. This was almost a mutation to me because the manmade environment in this country had always been rather introverted and less exhibitionistic. The outside had always reflected the inside and both shared the same aesthetic order.

However, what I found in the 1960s was quite different. The surfaces of the buildings were not always reflecting what was happening inside. Instead they were oriented to the outside. The surface of each building was a mirror reflecting the city itself, or, a membrane that wrapped you up in the city and so confirmed your orientation. The more active the urban surfaces, the more certain my obsession became.

One of the most deregulated downtown areas of Tokyo is Shinjuku, where two million commuters converge during the workday, and then entertain themselves in its myriad night spots after dark. Visually, the area is a *mélange*, with every imaginable use and building type compressed together around the immense and pulsating station. I had my first commissions to design two night entertainment buildings in Shinjuku; the Ichiban-kan (1969), and Niban-kan (1970). While I conceived both buildings to be site specific and particular to the client's requirements, I also applied intuitive discoveries relative to my design goal. I treated the building surface as a membrane 'wrapped around' the people on the street. Yet, one of the most memorable questions I received about these buildings outside Japan was, 'Why and how could the people in this neighbourhood allow you to design such buildings?'

Generally, the surface of a building reflects human concern with the mutual relationship between the outside and inside. Let me add another interesting experience of my own to prove this preoccupation.

Just before the Winter Olympic Games were held in Sapporo in 1972, my parents who were living in an old townhouse in the central district of the city asked my advice as an architect. Their eighty-year old wooden house looked a bit too shabby to exhibit itself on the main street, especially to foreign visitors and therefore, they eagerly wanted to refresh the exterior. My father first asked a local painter to repaint the external walls but they soon found that the wooden shingles were too weak to hold the new coat of paint. My proposal, after careful consideration, was to leave the existing external conditions of the house as they were and to put another membrane over it. Using ready-made aluminium shingles which were easily attached to ready-made stringers applied on site, I created a new external surface for my parents' house in less than two weeks. The shabby exterior had changed into a new aluminium wall with blue and white stripes which were intended to symbolise the nature of their seafood business.

With the extra coat, which also improved the noise and heat insulation, the house pleased my parents extremely. One thing happened, however, beyond their expectations. Judging from the new exterior walls, all the neighbours thought that my parents had built an entirely new building in two weeks and insisted on visiting the house. On entering they were even more surprised to discover that inside everything remained the same as before.

Metaphor

In the paradigmatic context in linguistic expression, the metaphor is a reliable way to read the meaning of a text, while in the syntagmatic context metonymy works better. In architectural rhetoric, where iconic and symbolic signs constitute the expression more than indexical ones, the metaphor tends to be emotional and illogical as it reflects the immanent and spontaneous perceptions

Instantly transforming facades; Kinichi-kan Department Store, Sapporo

of human senses. Therefore, it often loses motivation and increases the arbitrariness between the *signifier* and the *signified*. Yet, it also helps us search for hidden meanings in a 'discontinuous continuity' and reveals the meaning of architecture in a heterological world.

In the early 1970s, I became interested in 'defrosting' the frozen rhetoric of modern architecture. Instead of continuing to speak a universal architectural language without regard to the given place, I tried to discover the particular meanings of architecture within the culture at hand. In some of my work, I was rather intentionally attempting to reach more explicitly rhetorical solutions with the aid of metaphor.

Let me explain using some examples. The first is 'Hotel Beverly Tom' (1973), which has often been commented upon as a case of metaphorical rhetoric. The hotel is in Tomakomai, Hokkaido, the northernmost island of Japan. Facing the Pacific Ocean, the port city of Tomakomai was expected to become one of the leading industrial bases in the country. The population of 150,000 at that time, was expected to increase to 500,000 within a few years.

Hokkaido extends from 42-46 degrees latitude and belongs to the subarctic climate zone. The natural environment here is well preserved because of the island's low population density. Just outside the city boundary there are national parks with volcanoes, lakes and forests of conifers, which are visible from the city streets.

The site is located between the western edge of the city and the newly opened industrial zone, and also between the mountain scenery and the ocean view. Because of rapid population and industrial growth, the city's urban planning was not well implemented yet, and there was uncertainty about the further development of the city as a whole. Meanwhile, advanced automation and robotic industrialisation was taking place in the production areas. Mega-scale industrial and mechanical forms seemed to occupy the entire landscape and we could hardly find human activity on the streets and the waterfront.

My design goal for the hotel was to establish a definite and self-contained form in this very uncertain and inhospitable environment. Ignoring the super-scale and mechanistic forms of the industrial zone, I tried instead to design a building whose content expressed the human activities it contained. The only positive features within the surroundings that I could depend upon, were the distant views of the natural landscape and the numerous lights of the industrial zone after dark.

I chose the cylinder as the most appropriate form to express the building's self-containment. As I proceeded with the design, I began to feel that the cylinder by itself could be interpreted as part of the industrial landscape. This led me to design the roof as a transparent geodesic dome. Functionally, it shelters a roof garden on top of the hotel – another expression of human activity within the building and its connection to the larger natural setting of the region. In time, however the form of the building became an icon in the city, by acquiring its own explicit range of meanings. Except in a symbolic sense, these meanings are divorced from both the human content and its industrial context.

Another project from this 'metaphorical' period is the 'Pepsi-Cola Bottling Plant' in Mikasa, which was built in 1972. This is a circular building with a funnel-shaped roof, designed to be as transparent as possible, so the structure could merge with its natural environment. In Pepsi terms it symbolised the 'crisp refreshment' of the company's product.

The client, a Pepsi franchisee, was unnerved by the design, feeling it went against the 'Pepsi tradition'. The yellow roof and ceiling reflect the compromise we reached to preserve what they felt to be their corporate identity. An American critic finding the funnel-shape of the roof irrational for Hokkaido's snowy climate, commented that the building was symbolic of an industrial Japan dedicated to 'producing rationally irrational products'. Oddly enough, the form of a funnel grew out of functional considerations: the circulation of the building occurs around its outer ring to facilitate deliveries and shipments. The area immediately beside the building therefore had to be kept free from excess snow, ruling out a roof that pitched outward. Because the central plant of the building is located at the centre, it was possible to funnel the snow there and melt it with the heat from the boiler. Hence a funnel. So, once again, form follows function.

Or rather, metaphor follows function, because I did not begin with a preconceived metaphor in mind. I still believe that architects should not be preoccupied with metaphor but let it evolve in its own way and time from the design considerations they are grappling with. A metaphor can be ambiguous and multivalent, yet its meanings can often be accessible to the public in a way that buildings with more elitist and self-conscious architectural language can not.

Ideographic Architecture

Language is one of the most powerful tools of human communication. Each of the many languages around the world puts its own stamp on the culture in which it is spoken and written. Japanese is justly famous for its uniqueness. Among its many aspects, I am mostly concerned with the simple fact that the written language is ideographically oriented. The visual nature of its writing seems to be closely related to non-linguistic signs including architectural language.

In short, written Japanese is a hybrid. It is a combination of Japanese syllables and Kanji or Chinese characters. Kanji started as hieroglyphic characters during the Han Dynasty in China and developed into ideographic signs. From China it was exported to other Far Eastern countries and as a result, some gaps in signification developed from one region to the next. Kanji was imported to Japan along with Buddhism in the fifth century and has

been used throughout the centuries ever since. The number of Kanji being used in the country today is extensive. Japanese children learn two hundred characters by the end of kindergarten and, two thousand by the end of high-school. Daily papers use about two thousand, and a handy dictionary contains five thousand. Being ideographic and not phonographic, Chinese characters are difficult to read and there are many characters we do not know how to pronounce, although we still understand their meaning. Two Asians from different nations with different phonetic interpretations of Kanji can still communicate visually, while verbal conversation would not be possible.

Beside Kanji, there are fifty Japanese letters called *Kana*. These are phonetic signs which have two types of written style. One is *Kata Kana* used originally by men. The other is *Hira Kana*, a cursive style, which was developed later primarily for female use. Today this gender distinction of the original usage has been lost and *Kata Kana* is now used to phonetically transcribe foreign words. The situation is even more eclectic today, in as much as the Japanese are now in the habit of combining foreign letters with domestic letters and characters, and even coining new words between the two families. Thus the visual form of the Japanese language is hybrid and heterogeneous, just like the forms of architectural expression in the everyday environment.

Advancement in audio-visual technologies and inter-cultural-exchanges have made drastic changes in human communications in Japan today, as in other information societies. The basic pattern of communication in this country, however, having been structured for centuries by the particularity of the language, remains unchanged. It is safe to say that the most popular everyday form of daily communication in this country is the so-called 'from mind to mind' understanding. Often depicted by Westerners to be 'wordless, soundless, silent, indirect, ambiguous, inscrutable . . . and so on'.

Now the question is: how can architects cope with a sub-culture if they wish their designs to become as much a medium of communication as the medium of language in society? It is not an easy task to search for the right answer. I am somehow convinced, however, that the general public tends to read, or decode architects' messages in a similar fashion to reading words. Let me point out some instances from my own work.

One case is a hospital we designed in Sapporo, a northern Japanese city. The client was a neurosurgeon who wanted to build a clinic with 800 beds, the largest of its kind as a single clinic. Generally, health care in Japan has a duality and people depend on both Western and Eastern medicines. Our client was 100 per cent Western educated and adopted advanced instruments for his surgical procedures from the beginning. The basic communication between doctors and patients seemed lacking, however, because of the insufficient welfare policy of the nation. Our solution for the hospital intended to realise architectural spaces where

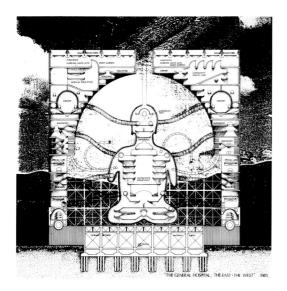

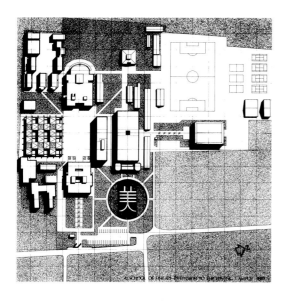

ABOVE and CENTRE: *General Hospital: East and West*
BELOW: *Preliminary scheme for Building No 10, Musashino Art University*

communication between the two sides could be recreated and maintained. In order to illustrate our intention, I made the proposal with the title 'General Hospital: East and West', with the following notes:

In the East the universe develops within the body, while in the West the body exists within the structure of the universe. Therefore Eastern medicine has developed insights into body and spirit by analogy establishing its own psychosomatic order. Western medicine, for its part, has advanced the scientific understanding of the human organism by homology. The aim of this hospital is to bridge these two worlds in order to secure their co-operation.

The building consists of the two forms; the internal Statue and the surrounding Cube. The Statue has all necessary facilities inside for the outpatients. Before entering they can easily find the quickest access to the appropriate medical department by simply identifying exactly the same portion of the Statue as that of their ailing body. The expression of the Statue is bisexual and double-faced, like the Janus of ancient Rome. By locating the Statue on the east-west axis, we can provide separate entrances for men and women on each face, while emergency care could enter from the top. The bodily and facial expression apparent to the outside is full of tranquillity, so that. . . people might consider the Statue as the Yakushi Nyorai, or the Buddha of Medicine. In fact some Japanese today still travel through the inside of the Great Buddha in Nara to pray for recovery and good health.

The Cube, on the other hand, maximises functions for diagnosis and treatment of patients. Here the capable physicians play their roles and use advanced instruments at their highest level. Its architectural expression should stay within the univalent language of modernism.

The Tubes which are made of pneumatic shafts with vacuum pumps link the Statue to the Cube, or the patients' demands to the doctors' care. From the outside the whole entity may look like the arms of the Thousand Armed Kwannon, the Goddess of Mercy. Visitors would worship the hospital always with wishes for good health and long life.

In this visionary scheme, an architectural statement was created in an ideographic manner. My ultimate goal was to express a confluence of opposite architectural meanings figurative and abstract, solid and transparent, analogy and homology in a single statement that proclaimed the paradoxical situation existing today in the communication between doctors and patients.

The second example is less visionary or utopian. For Building No 10 of Musashino Art Institute, where I teach, I proposed a form that resembles the Chinese character for beauty, which is also the school's symbol. In a naive way I hoped that this would remind students to be more aware of their campus as a physical setting.

The students accepted the project but it was rejected by the administration. As built the project is more syntactic – an extension of the existing building it adjoins. Yet the first idea had an impact, because the form of the character suggested the possibility of an internal mall and atrium between the new and older buildings – a space where teachers and students could meet and interact. Edward de Bono has also noted this phenomenon, that a word (or character) chosen arbitrarily can trigger associations that can lead to a creative response.

Oxymoron

Every culture maintains its identity by preserving its traditions and following new trends. In Japan the gap between old and new is so pronounced and tangible that any cultural identity seems double-coded, overlapping rather than congruent.

Taste and lifestyle in Japan run on two tracks – Japanese and Western. We call them *wa* and *yo*, and together, they intrude into every aspect of daily life. The results are sometimes contradictory, sometimes eclectic and serendipitous. Only an anthropologist can keep track of the resulting duality.

The average Japanese man spends his day in *yo-fuku* (Western clothes) then changes to *wa-fuku* (traditional Japanese clothes) when he gets home. He keeps his *yo-fuku* in a *yo-tansu* (cabinet) and his *wa-fuku* in a *wa-tansu*. He has *wa-shoku* (Japanese food) for his breakfast and *yo-shoku* for lunch at his office. His dinner is more eclectic but is usually served in a *wa-shitu* (traditional Japanese room), seated on the floor. Later, talking to his children, he will have to decide if his son should study *wa-gakki* (traditional Japanese instrument) or *yo-gakki* at school, and if his daughter should wear *wa-fuku* or *yo-fuku* at her school party.

This has been going on since the Meiji Restoration. When it took power in 1868, the Meiji government instituted an all-encompassing edict called *wa kon yo sai* or 'Japanese Spirit upon Western Intelligence'. Every aspect of life was affected by this cultural sea change, including the built environment. Traditional Japanese architecture lost its official sanction, and its use and place in society were limited and defined. Thus a duality of styles was set in motion that architects have had to cope with as an added complication to modernisation and the creative process.

Some architects have coped by neglecting or even attacking the 'enemy' of *wa* and *yo*. Others sought a tenuous integration by excluding, in the name of consistency, those aspects of each that they deemed inharmonious. My approach, which is more inclusive but no less demanding, has been to try to hold opposing styles and meanings in equilibrium without compromising either of them. Borrowing from the terms of language, this is the oxymoron, bracketing together opposite or incongruous meanings without placing anything between them to hide their incompatibility.

Japan is awash with oxymorons, especially in our maxims and proverbs, such as: 'a loser is a winner', 'make haste slowly', 'an open secret', 'skilful awkwardness', and so on. Perhaps this is because our country is so rooted in consensus – holding opposites in equilibrium is just part of everyday life and much may be understood without having to be stated.

One of my architectural statements for the oxymoronic approach, or coping with the duality of the styles of *wa* and *yo*, was the 'General Hospital: East and West', as stated before. As another realised work with a similar inclination, let me turn to the 'Renaissance' building in Kyoto.

A very old city, Kyoto has many national treasures within its borders. To protect them and its historic fabric, the city has enacted very restrictive local regulations and design controls: no vertical expression, a limited colour palette, no neon signage and so on. The external facade of the Renaissance consists of granite walls, designed in the traditional Western manner with the granite set in courses, over a light-weight framework of aluminium pipes, articulated like the traditional Japanese timber frame in a temple. My intention was not to reconcile these two traditions, but to express the visual duality one finds in Kyoto – a duality that has characterised the city over much of its 1,200 year history as it has had to absorb successive and often contradictory cultural influences.

Time

In my daily life in Tokyo, I often lose the memory of the constituting elements of a street, no matter how close I feel to it. For instance, when finding a construction site or discovering a new empty space along the street, I can hardly recall what was there before and I cannot recollect it. It is sad that not only buildings but also other things as well seem to disappear. Objects for which I used to have particular feelings, such as a neighbour's mail box, a thick wooden electric pole or a man-hole cover with a relief, get easily lost and cannot be revived in my memory. The main reason for this amnesia, however, lies not necessarily in my ability to retain memory, but in the fact that the streetscape keeps changing beyond the capacity of human memory.

Buildings in Japan are constantly in flux. The transience of the built environment in this country was established long ago in its traditional customs. The best known example is the rebuilding and relocation of the Ise Shinto Shrine every twenty years, a ritual which is still observed today. Originally the reason for the reconstruction was simply the limited durability of its wooden materials, but later the custom gained symbolic meaning in connection to Shintoism. Similarly, the new Tokyo City hall, the second tallest building complex in this country at present, was built only thirty-four years after the former City Hall had been completed by the same architect. Both buildings were selected and realised through an architectural design competition which requested the architects to build a symbolic structure and everlasting monument. (I tried to help preserve the former building but the idea was not welcomed by the city authority or the architect.) The same thing happens to more ordinary buildings, including many that I have designed; they keep changing or disappear as victims of intense land speculation.

Is there any particular time-perception that can be attributed to the people of this country? In this respect the critics' remarks are worthy of attention and offer some clues. According to their analysis of paintings for example, the three-dimensional representations that first appeared in Japanese paintings were basically different from those of the Renaissance. The Yamatoe (townscape drawing) of the Edo period was rendered more or less in an isometric way, while the scenography of the Renaissance was drawn in very stable perspective. In the latter the viewer has a clear position which is suggested by well-defined vanishing points. In the former, however, the position of the subject is lost from the picture, or dispersed into every object in the scene so that every represented item has its own subjective position. The Renaissance perspective is visual, while the Japanese representation is *situational*. In the visually stable perspective the sense of time is frozen and everything presented belongs to the same framework or idea. However in the Japanese painting, time is constantly shifting and the movement itself is described so that every item seems to have its own course of time. It is as if we make a series of sequential images depicting motion using time-lapse photography.

I have a similar impression of the multiple images of some traditional pieces of sculpture. Why did they put so many arms on the same body (the Goddess of a Thousand Arms), or so many faces to the same head (the Multi-faced Kwannon)? My interpretation is that the viewer or worshipper could select any combination of meanings from the variations of arms, or of facial expressions depending upon the viewer's situation. The basic intent was to signify time differential in these variations of expression, and therefore tangible and symbolic messages are more important than aesthetic.

In literature, a similar tendency could be found. A well-known translator, who has translated many Japanese literary works, including contemporary ones, into English, mentioned that it is very difficult to locate the subject in the Japanese sentence. This is because the subject is often missed or even moving from one place to the other simultaneously. This is true in daily conversation as well where we can express ourselves using many different first person pronouns or even by omitting the subject altogether. This nature of the Japanese language reflects the same tendency as paintings and sculptures do, that is the lack of a fixed standing point, or the instability of the subject, allowing the surrounding objects to obtain as much significance as the subject.

What I am saying is that the heterogeneity of expression in various Japanese fields seems to be closely related to people's sensitivity to time, which allows objects to share the same importance of existence as the subject. With this observation in mind, I have conceptualised some projects in which *space* was intended to correspond with *time*, or *space* which flows as time passes by. In my search for the right answer to cope with the heterogeneous environment, the changing space seemed to be one of the most appropriate solutions.

I have designed several projects that try to replicate this specifically Japanese attitude toward time. One of them is Atelier Indigo, my studio in Sapporo, built in 1976, and named after my older daughter. It is a simple reinforced concrete frame structure with wooden cladding. The ground floor workshop is a large open volume with storage spaces on both sides to hold furniture and other household goods. In this way, it was possible to start with a clean slate once in a while, rearranging things to suit our changing needs. The roof of the studio is a kind of terrace dominated by eight hinged cubes, each 2.2 x 2.2 metres. In good weather these are constantly being changed by people as they 'make their own time' on the roof. To passers-by, the roof must seem both like a clock and a barometer, measuring the changing whims of the occupants as well as the hours of the day. In winter, when snow covers the roof, the cubes hibernate and time and space are finally frozen until the spring thaw.

Another example of a practical project where time introduces subtle variations is the interior design of a shoe store, called 'Shu Pub'. Here, my efforts concentrated on the packaging of the merchandise. The shoes are packed according to style with more than one size to each box, therefore the box could be designed with a single coloured pattern which is independent of the style. A variety of colours, code marks and other information are also printed on the surface of the boxes so that the sales assistants can easily identify different merchandise. The installation of shelves to store the shoe boxes exposes the stock to the customers as a vividly coloured wall. With sales and enquiries, the wall of boxes is simultaneously renewed, refreshing the colours and patterns with discontinuous continuity. The visual effect infinitely changes.

Urban Context

Is it possible to switch the context of an urban environment entirely as we can rewrite the text? Lately in this heterogeneous environment of Tokyo, I notice dimly that the text of the city is changing. The context of the city appears to be shifting from the paradigmatic to the syntagmatic; in other words, I can now observe more new 'neighbours' than 'brothers' around me.

One remarkably noticeable transformation is happening on the city's streets. Many that used to look confused and disordered with no sense of continuous streetscape now appear to have some quality of continuity. The random gaps between buildings are being filled in and the facade along the street has become a continuously solid plane. The edge of the buildings, which used to be extremely uneven and irregular, has now become somewhat ordered with a more regulated skyline. In addition, pedestrian malls and shopping arcades are becoming more popular in urban districts with tree circles, stone pavements, imported street furniture and other tools for beautification. The streets are becoming real living places, as far as I can read from recent phenomena.

One of the major reasons that streets are gaining a sense of order and continuity is attributable to the economy. The Japanese economy has been essentially based upon the land value, and the city is the stage where, like on a stock market, ownership is traded. During the period of the so-called 'bubble economy', the drama of land ownership dealings reached a maximum point, sometimes kicking certain inhabitants off a site, evicting unprotected tenants, or subdividing empty lots into smaller pieces. Since properties fronting streets with good commercial potential were of great value to developers they built up these sites to the maximum total floor ratio permitted by the building codes. No matter how tiny the lot, the empty spaces were appraised like diamonds and built up. Consequently, building density along these streets has increased with the streetscape gaining the appearance of unbroken solid plane with smaller yet taller buildings lined up wall to wall. People began referring to these structures as 'pencil buildings'.

As presented here, I have designed a few pencil buildings both in Tokyo and Osaka. In designing a building on a small site, I recommended that the land owner join the site with that of its neighbours in order to increase the site and building area and thus, the business opportunity. Unfortunately financial reasons have always proved to be more serious than the environmental interest. In most cases the buildings were occupied by rental offices with some additional multiple use functions, and had the typical demands for the optimum rental ratio and space efficiency. Both the owner and the tenants required the buildings to face the street with identical expressions. My experiences in designing pencil buildings may explain how streets are getting more continuously built up and giving different images from the previous appearance.

However this phenomenon is happening only along major streets. Remarkably the back streets remain unchanged. This duality between the front and the back has increased more than ever before, with almost the same contrast that prevails between a spot-lit stage and the hidden backstage in a theatre. Here the older fabric of the city still retains its vitality and the inherent context is firmly alive in the deeper dimension.

Fata Morgana

Although Japan is surrounded by the sea, its cities have until very recently turned their backs to the water. While there were harbours to facilitate trade, the waterfront in general was thought of as a *cordon sanitaire* to protect the city from its human and natural enemies. Public access to the waterfront was long prohibited, and official acceptance of the idea that it could be a public place and amenity is only very recent.

These restrictions made it impossible for people to see a city like Tokyo 'at a glance' from across the water. As a result urban identity could not be given by a total view but by the experience of fragmented parts and symbolic elements. The image of the city segmented depending on which fragments of the whole entity a person could see. The city was experienced in the same manner as the three blind men describing the elephant according to the part they touched; the trunk, the tail or the ear. Opening the waterfront has allowed for the first time, the emergence of the panoramic view of the city making it possible for the whole to be seen. As Tokyo grows taller, the distant views of the city across the water have become more dramatic and important. In consequence, the architects of these new buildings have begun to take the 'skyline view' more and more into account in their work.

One of my recent projects is the Tokyo Port Terminal on Tokyo harbour that serves as the gateway to the city for visiting cruise ships. While working on this project I could observe the rapidly changing skyline of the city from a distance for several years. During this period many high-rise buildings have appeared like so many mushrooms on the horizon. A large suspension bridge was also built to connect the developing waterfront area with the city's existing centres.

One of my hopes for the design of the Terminal was to relate it to this larger emerging context. I guessed that, with the city becoming more homogeneous in its outward appearance, I could predict its future development with some accuracy. In time though I began to doubt that this was possible. Although the visual entity seems to be changing in its context, the end of this change is still unpredictable and full of uncertainty. This experience confirmed my sense that Tokyo's underlying urban structure is immutable – an indestructible paradigm that has guided the city's development from the early 1600s. It seems as deeply rooted in our particular culture as the structure of our language. Above it floats the changing signs of the visible city, still heterogeneous and unpredictable.

Ichiban-kan

Tokyo 1967–69

Niban-kan

Tokyo 1968–70

The two buildings, in close proximity to each other, are located in Kabuki-cho, the night spot in Shinjuku, which is one of the largest downtown areas of the metropolis. (Since the New Tokyo City Hall was completed in 1991, Shinjuku has also become the centre of urban politics.) In the 1960s when these buildings were designed, the area was spontaneously developing from a residential to a commercial district dominated primarily by night entertainment. Consequently the residential atmosphere was totally lost, and the area fell into disorder. Today, more than two million commuters are reported to come through Shinjuku daily, many of them regularly patronising the more than 3,000 bars or night clubs, and 200 cafes located here.

The Ichiban-kan (Building No 1) and Niban-kan (Building No 2) were planned for the same client, primarily for the purpose of night entertainment and built one after the other within a year. The Ichiban-kan consists of eight floors above street level and two basements, each of which has eight small rental spaces for bars, night clubs, cafes and game rooms. Two elevators and one stairway link the floors. The vertical circulation is designed as an extension of the public street, so that guests can enter the building without an interruption. The glass walls covering the slanted front sides of the building, and the black and white bands painted on the outside walls are used as dominant signs so that guests can easily identify the building from a distance. The half-mirror glass walls are designed to perform fascinating animation with light and a range of visual illusions, as they reflect the surrounding cityscape throughout the day, while at night the electric illumination inside

renders the glass walls transparent when seen from the outside, with the interior spaces appearing as if in a kaleidoscope.

In the case of the Niban-kan, the owner wanted to run his own businesses, restaurants, night clubs, sauna baths and games corners. In order to respond to Ichiban-kan, the surface of the building is painted with polychromatic colours sensitive to lighting. The external materials were initially required to be cost-saving, and made of exposed concrete and metal sheets which need repainting for protection every five years. A colourful 'supergraphic' on the surface was proposed for every repainting, and the graphic designer Kiyoshi Awazu was asked to do the first pattern. Five years later it was revised by another designer. Besides maintenance, the process of painting and changing the supergraphic images was intended to keep up with drastic changes in the surrounding environment.

Such a solution for these buildings would not have been possible anywhere else but Kabuki-cho, where the order of the environment, if any, is deeply hidden behind the visual disorder of phenomena, and where people can live an active and autonomous life in confusion, while enjoying individual freedom.

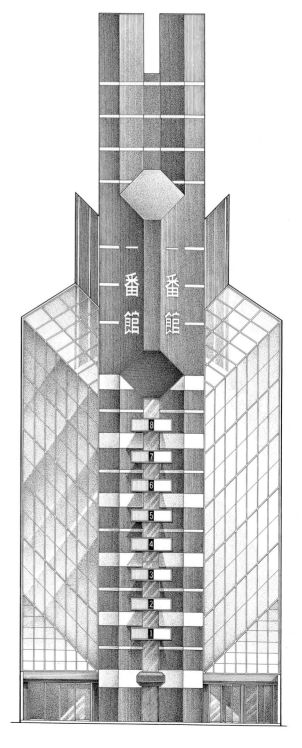

OPPOSITE: *Street scene with Niban-kan in the foreground and Ichiban-kan to the right*

RIGHT: *Facade elevation of the Ichiban-kan*

Atrium, Niban-kan

Stairwell, Niban-kan

Atrium, Ichiban-kan

BELOW: *Rendered elevational diagram of Niban-kan;*
Niban-kan after repainting; aerial view of Ichiban-kan
and Niban-kan

OPPOSITE: *Niban-kan with original*
supergraphic

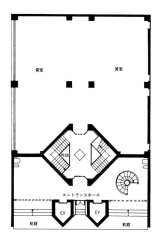 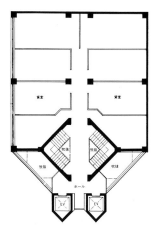 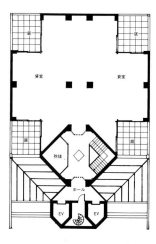

Peter Popham in his book, *Tokyo: The City at the End of the World*, commented as follows: *Like the* yakuza, *the 'gangsters' who own and run Kabuki-cho's porno shops and sex rackets, it's beyond the pale of the straight world, but it is held in check by rigid rules and conventions of its own. And those rules are not significantly different from those of mainstream Japanese society. As a result, Kabuki-cho is rough, lurid, noisy and goes on all night – yet in essentials it's not different from a regular Tokyo main street. It's just a sort of comically exaggerated version of that.*

Like the city's more conventional main streets, Kabuki-cho is the creation of a society whose crucial divisions are not those of occupation or class.

For in Japan's increasingly egalitarian society, in which, nonetheless, nobody is actually equal to anybody else – not even pairs of identical twins – harmony of the Western sort cannot come to pass. In its place is the intense yet rigidly controlled rivalry graphically illustrated in the narrow and smelly backstreets of Kabuki-cho.

The section of Kabuki-cho [where Takeyama's Ichiban-kan and Niban-kan Buildings stand] is full of bar buildings, structures of five or six or more stories crammed with small pubs, clubs, and 'snacks' from top to bottom, separated by inches and single-mindedly devoted to shouting each other down. Ichiban-kan has forty-nine bars, yes forty-nine, distributed through eight floors, and joins in the scrummage in deadly earnest. The difference is that, whereas the others are merely streetwise, Ichiban-kan is intelligent,

too. Takeyama has looked hard and long at what his building must do, and what it need not bother to do, and the result is genuinely original.

First of all, the building must make a splash. It absolutely must not merge into its surroundings. It must shout its head off. Takeyama achieves this with a zebra-striped form clad in iron and glass which looks like an exercise in avant-garde origami.

The rival bar buildings on either side have conventional entrance foyers and elevator halls, like low-rent office buildings. Why bother? What boozer wants to be reminded of his workplace? In function a bar building like this is essentially an up-ended Golden Gai alley, like the one we passed through earlier as it was waking up. As in Golden Gai, all the snugness and luxury is inside the individual bars; outside is outside, whether it's the street or eight floors up, and thus Ichiban-kan has an aperture rather than an entrance, and no front door. Squeeze in, stroll up. The huge areas of window on either side of the elevators help to reinforce the sensation that this is a street in the air.

Finally, there is the treatment of the signs. The bars are the raison-d'être *of these buildings, and accordingly the signs advertising them ought to be the focus of attention; yet on most of the nearby buildings they seem to have been stuck on just anyhow, as afterthoughts. At Ichiban-kan, they fit snugly into the gap between the two structural columns at the front, and the chevrons of the windows rush down towards them like diving birds. They are the centre of the design, all the rest converges on them.*

They also help us to appreciate what is

lively and different about Japan's new architecture – or so Takeyama believes. His own Ichiban-kan is one of the best demonstrations of the theory.

ABOVE, L to R: *Ichiban-kan ground floor plan; typical floor plan; eighth floor plan*

BELOW: *Ichiban-kan*

OPPOSITE: *Worm's eye axonometric of Ichiban-kan*

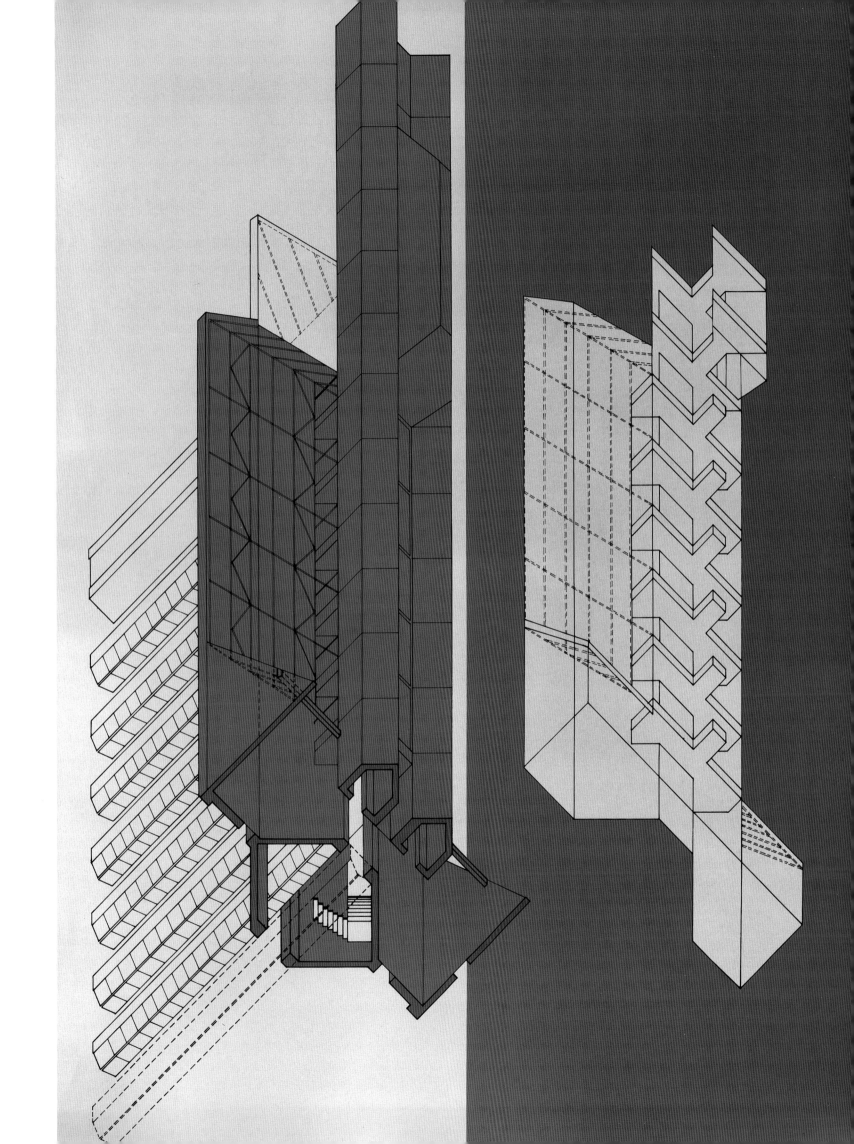

Labor Union Hall

Fuji Heavy Industries
Omiya City 1968–70

The site was in a corner of the existing factory complex of Subaru Automobile Manufacturing (Fuji Heavy Industries) outside Tokyo. In order to express symbolically the nature of a labour union as a social body, it was intended that the external expression would come from the spatial relations generated within the building, while simultaneously incorporating in the interior spaces the environmental elements generated outside. To achieve this, the outer shell was dissolved and left in an apparent state of incompletion. Takeyama has attempted a refreshing reversal of a hard, thick, and completely ordered shell enclosure that often tends to stylise the interior in terms of exterior volume.

Full-height spaces, glass-membrane walls, and subtle modulations of story heights are major devices to germinate more abundant space relations among the upper and lower levels. In order to go beyond the simple connection by difference of levels, and to develop an organic connection among the individual rooms and the multi-purpose auditorium (capacity 400 people), the glass membranes and the full-height space bind together the large corner entrance lobby, the cantilevered, balcony-style corridors, and the top-level linear foyer, while simultaneously projecting each of these elements to the exterior of the building. Thus the internal human activities, being seen from outside, become part of exterior expression, like a stage in the theatre.

By shutting off the private rooms and the auditorium itself from the exterior as much as possible, with no spatial relations between them, it was hoped to increase the occupants' control over their privacy. These two zones – the exposed glass-covered connecting area and the enclosed independent private spaces – are symbolically related by means of colour scheme. The auditorium is rendered largely in black and gold, the open glazed section in white, and the private rooms in any of seven colours, which dominate their interiors and spill out through the doors and windows to create a sense of symbolic, non-ornamental connection between the individual elements and the total composition.

Exploded axonometric

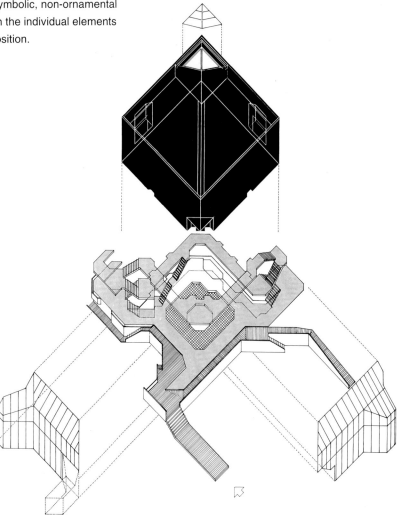

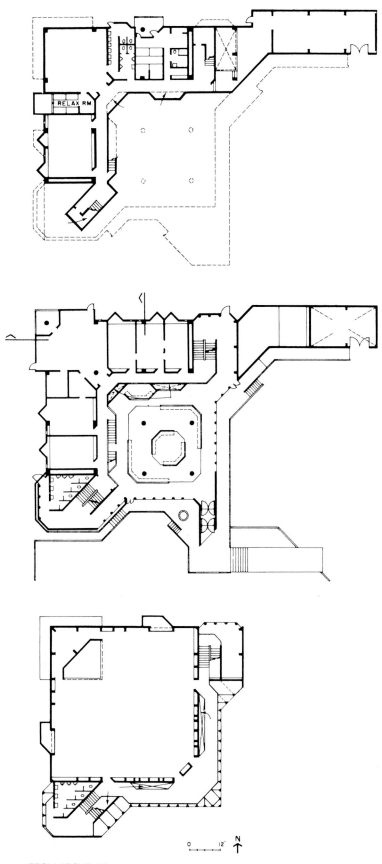

FROM ABOVE: *Mezzanine plan;*
ground floor plan; first floor plan

Shu-Pub Store

Tokyo 1970–80

Shu-Pub is a shoe store chain which sells mainly men's shoes. Stores have been installed at more than ten places in downtown Tokyo.

In the interior design of the first Shu-Pub, the creative efforts concentrated on the packaging of the merchandise instead of the interior space as a whole. Knowing that a range of shoe sizes could fit in the same box, the package was designed with a single independent pattern, but also with associative links to others. Different colours, codes and other information were printed and stamped on the surface of the boxes so that the sales persons could easily identify the merchandise. The only installations are shelves to store the shoe boxes. Instead of hiding the merchandise in a rear stockroom, the solution was to expose all of its stock to the customers. With the ongoing sales activities the walls, made out of boxes, keep refreshing their colours and patterns, in a 'discontinuous continuity', from time to time. The space remains the same but its visual effect changes constantly, like pieces of a mosaic which can be substituted without altering the whole composition.

Interior axonometric

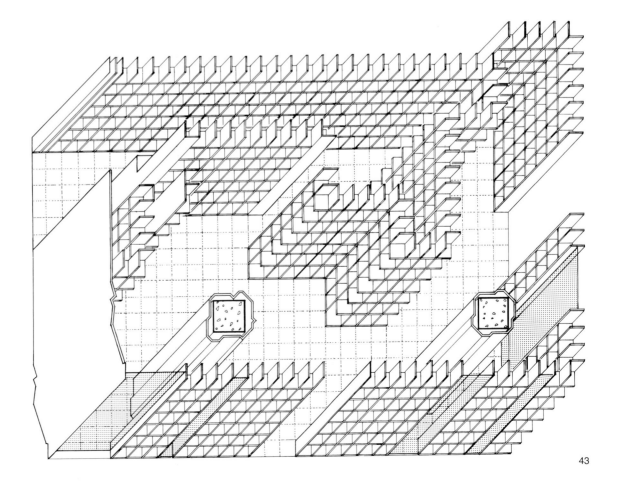

43

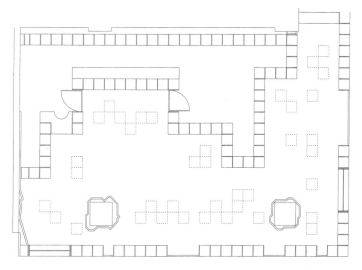

BELOW LEFT: *Floor plan*

Iwakura Office

Tomakomai City, Hokkaido 1969–71

The building was the home office of the Iwakura Gumi Construction Company, a large-scale lumber dealer. The total personnel of the combined organisation is 2,000 people but the number of employees actually working at the home offices was 50. As the management and organisation of the company was expected to grow more multi-faceted and complicated, with a growing number of staff, provisions were made to accommodate the excess personnel in two tower additions planned for the future.

The basic intention was to devise a 'street' within the building, or to permit a part of the private domain to function as public space. Although at present the axis leading from the road in front of the building, up the entrance stairs, and to the courtyard garden ends in a cul-de-sac, in the future it would penetrate the rear of the building and connect to the garden on the backside. This 'street' within the building is open to anyone who wants to enter. All major rooms or spaces open from it and draw their natural lighting from its skylight. At present, the first floor is occupied by the computer room and conference room/salon space, the second by the main offices, and the third by the executive offices. In the future, the function of these spaces will probably change.

This building is designed with no views of the outside. At the outset of the design it was impossible to predict whether the adjacent sites would be built upon at any point in the future, and so outside views were not considered. Consequently, the street within the building became the outside space. The public aspect of the enclosed street is deliberately emphasised and completely isolated from all exterior scenery by means of blank outside walls.

Design efforts were concentrated on the search for a basic connection between architecture and the city by re-evaluating the relationship between public and private domains in one of the newly opened local industrial areas in Tomakomai.

Axonometric showing internal street

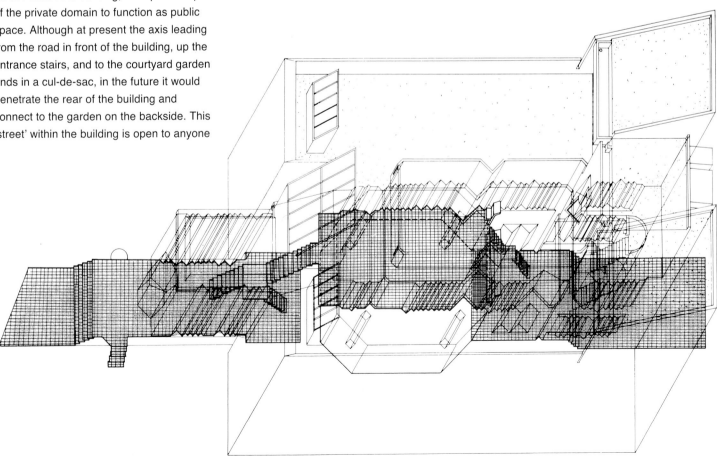

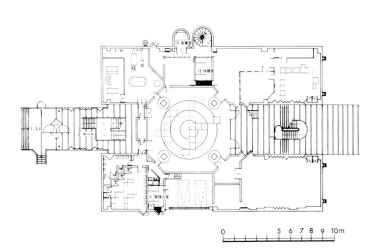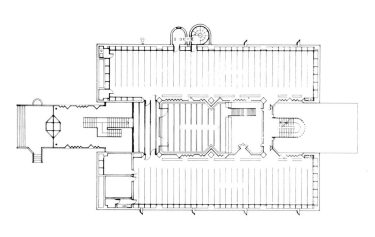

0　　　　5 6 7 8 9 10m

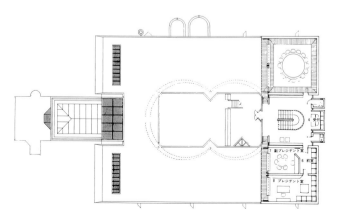

OPPOSITE BELOW, L to R:
Ground floor plan; first floor plan

LEFT: *Second floor plan*

Pepsi-Cola Bottling Plant

Mikasa, Hokkaido 1972

The Plant stands at the outskirts of the town of Mikasa, which was once a centre of coal mining on Hokkaido, the northernmost island in the Japanese archipelago. The building faces a major national highway which crosses Mikasa.

The main programme called for the installation of two production lines canning Pepsi-Cola, with the possibility of future expansion. The prominence of the site means that, in addition to the thirty employees of the plant, an indefinite number of people are coming into contact with it as they pass by on the highway. Consequently, while fulfilling the functional requirements of the factory, the environmental effect and the setting of the plant in the distinctive, Hokkaido landscape were important design elements. Accordingly, the building was designed as a brilliant, light-reflecting glass cylinder with an inverted conical roof which appears to float above it. The painted yellow colour on both the roof and ceiling were the proposal of the clients who considered the colour to be a symbol of Pepsi-Cola.

Around the building, as part of the landscaping, an artificial mound was created to block the views of the working zone from the highway. Thus, only the upper part of the building which responds to the natural surrounding is visible from a distance. The three-quarters-cylindrical body, with a diameter of 59 metres and height of 19.5 metres, is supported by thirty-seven sets of radially-arranged space frames of steel pipes, each with a diameter of 165 millimetres. The production space for the Pepsi Plant (with an average speed of 500 cans per minute) is within this part of the building. The inverted cone roof has a pitch of 30 degrees. Its lowest section is outfitted with a heating device, directly con-nected to the boiler room below, to melt the accumulated snow in winter. This prevents snow from falling from the roof onto the outdoor work space around the building.

The intention with the design was to establish dramatically direct relations between the inside and the outside of the building, and further, between the artificial, or mechanical, and the organically natural.

Structural diagram of radial space frame

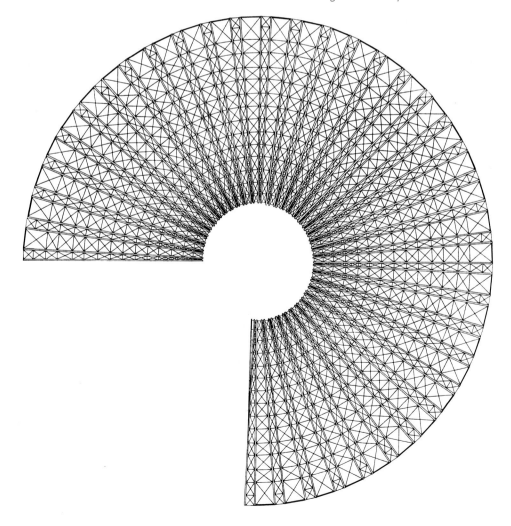

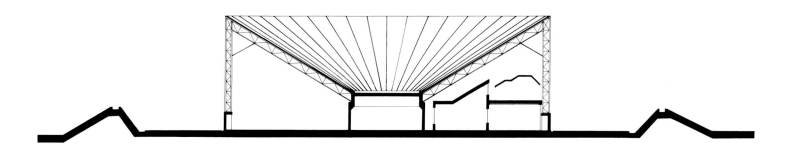

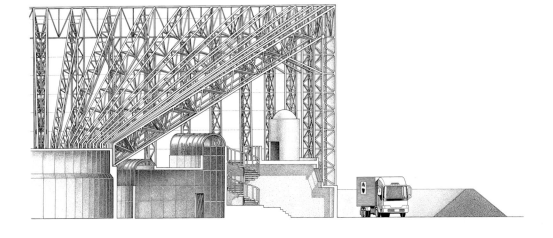

ABOVE: *Section*

LEFT: *Cross-sectional elevation through circulation zone*

OPPOSITE ABOVE: *Proposed site development plan*

OPPOSITE BELOW: *Simplified elevation*

OPPOSITE RIGHT: *Exploded axonometric*

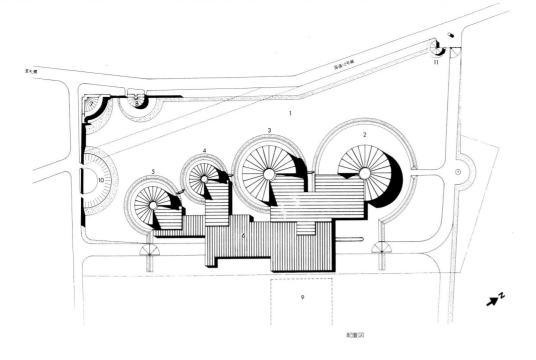

配置図

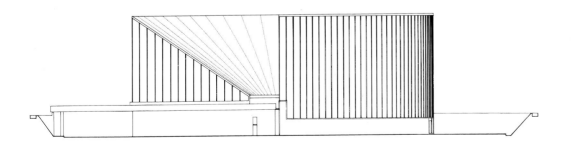

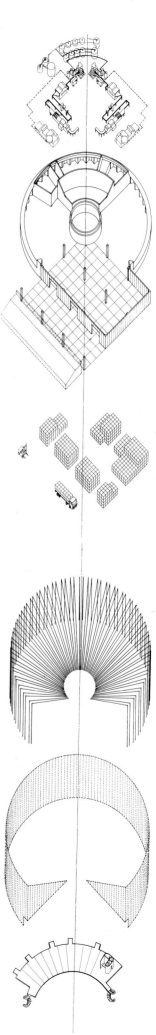

Hotel Beverly Tom

Tomakomai City, Hokkaido 1971–73

The Hotel is located in an industrial region at the east end of the business district of Tomakomai. Adjacent to the building is the harbour, which cuts inwards from the sea, while a national highway runs in front of the site. The building is at the intersection of the highway with an industrial road leading to the port. Since this is a reclaimed area, greenery is scarce. Nevertheless, about four kilometres inland from the bay there is a forest that covers the foothills of Mount Tarumae. Although the town originally developed in a linear pattern along the shore, rapid and dramatic expansion inland is expected in the future.

Three-quarters of the cylindrical tower, defined and protected by a relatively solid wall, face the industrial district. The quarter cylinder opening looks towards the peak of Mt Tarumae. At night, looking out from their windows, people can see the lights of the industrial zone spreading out like a carpet on the ground. During the day, through the open side of the cylinder and from the corridors, which are on the inside of the circular plan, the beautiful greenery and the mountains themselves become visible. This design solution, however, is more than a mere blending of the natural and artificial environments. As both of these environments invade the building, they come into conflict with each other and emerge with a different quality. Actually there is no clear architectural form that can represent the intersecting realm that exists between the worlds of nature on one side and the inhuman industrial zone on the other.

Takeyama has attempted to use a phallic symbol to play this role in the hotel, with variations placed modestly throughout the building. However, the most basic (and largest) symbol is the form of the tower itself. The phallic metaphor signifies the aggressive perseverance of the human body, even in a dramatically changing environment which lacks any human presence. Takeyama wanted the symbol to implant itself into the deep levels of the brain, to the level of concealed non-notational response and was eager to see to what extent he could give an ideographic form to emotions.

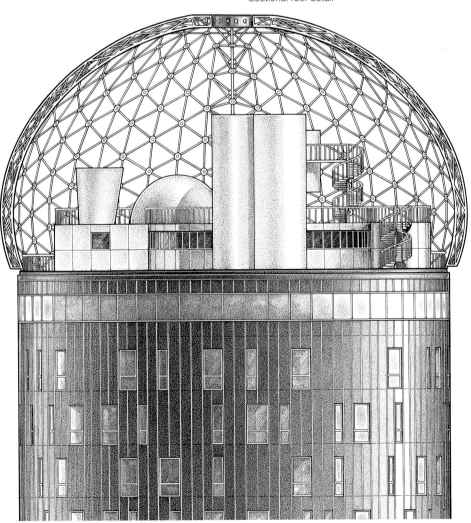

Sectional roof detail

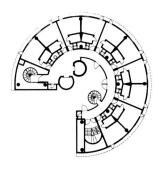

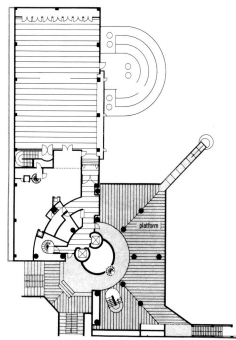

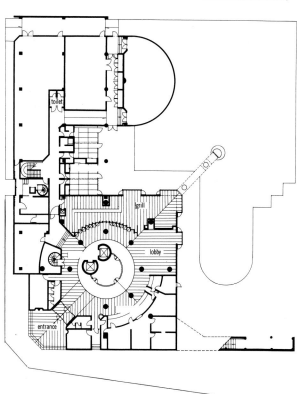

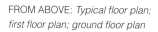

FROM ABOVE: *Typical floor plan;*
first floor plan; ground floor plan

Iwakura Residence
Tomakomai City, Hokkaido 1971–73

This project was designed and built to meet the needs of three related families, who required their own homes to conduct life independently, while also needing a place where all the families could get together. The site was adjacent to a lumber yard and factory owned by the same clients. It was expected that at a later date this lumber yard would be relocated to another part of the city, and that a larger scale project for the entire site could then be implemented. Therefore, this residence for the three families was considered to be a test model for future development.

Takeyama's design goal was to permit freedom to each individual housing unit without sacrificing the total order of syntax. The whole complex consists of two major syntactic elements; the 'corridors' and the 'rooms', both of which were manufactured and pre-finished in the client's factory.

The corridors are comprised of 1.2 metre-wide concrete frames with connected pairs of posts supporting a system of box-beams on top and foundation beams below. The corridors function as the passage, piping and mechanical space, and also divide the main living rooms. The main living rooms are placed between the corridors, and are combined with open courtyards. These rooms are placed on the ground level, but if required could be arranged on the second floor. While the corridors are constructed of concrete, the rooms are all of wood, a material readily available in Hokkaido, and whose structure could be prefabricated locally in the client's factory.

In future development, when the total plan was envisioned, the corridors were intended to be public passages while the rooms would respond to each private domain. The main idea in the final planning was to realise 'an urban village' which could encourage mutual dependence among inhabitants without spoiling each individual amenity, by eliminating unnecessary 'in-between' spaces of low-rise houses and achieving a more cohesive habitat of low-rise and high density.

The Iwakura Residence is the forerunner to a larger scheme, the High-density, Low-rise Housing Project, which Takeyama designed in 1973. This diagram shows the conceptual site formation of 'corridors' and 'rooms' in this project

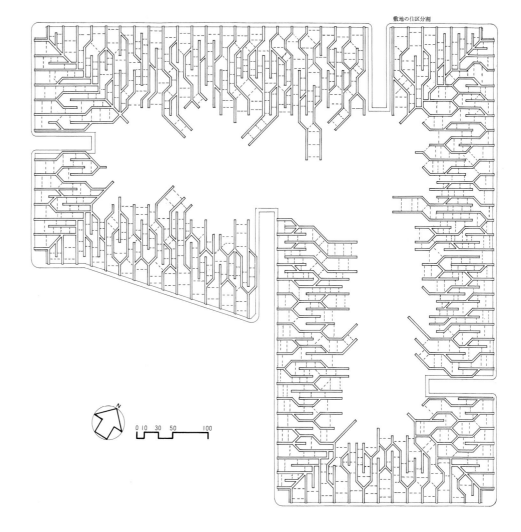

敷地の住区分割

0 10 30 50 100

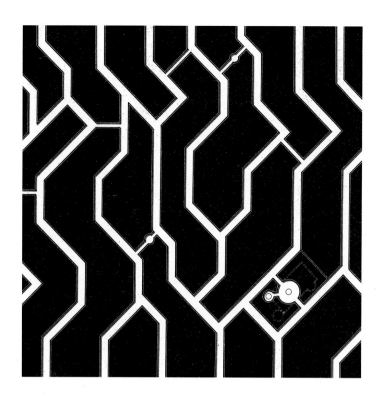

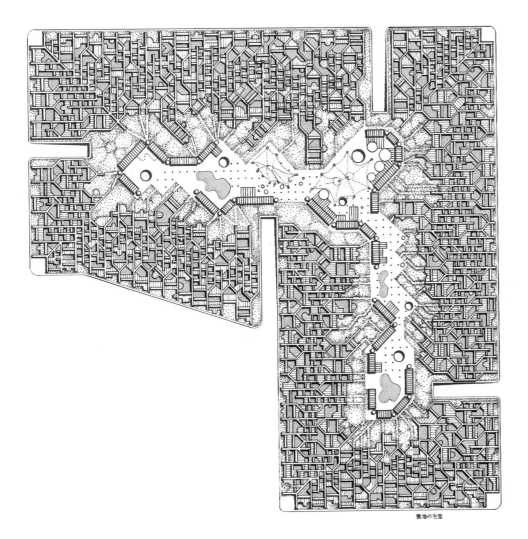

散地の生態

OPPOSITE ABOVE (L to R):
*Conceptual diagram of 'trench';
conceptual diagram of 'corridor'
(High-density Low-rise Housing
Project)*

LEFT: *Conceptual site plan
showing use of corridors and
open spaces (High-density Low-
rise Housing Project)*

Atelier Indigo

Sapporo, Hokkaido 1974–76

This small building is Takeyama's own studio, which was produced and built by members of his office, and which, after its completion, was named after the architect's daughter, Indigo. The site is in the city of Sapporo, the capital of Hokkaido with a population of nearly two million, and the birthplace of Takeyama, where he also maintains a part of his own practice.

The concrete structural framework was cast on-site and the walls clad with local pine logs. The main floor is meant to be a universal space, usually as studio and occasionally as an event hall with invited guest speakers and performers. The large storage spaces on both sides, behind the demountable walls, function like the back stage of a theatre and support various activities in the studio. All the furniture, including working booths, is designed to be easily moved and dismantled.

On top of the building, a large 'Cube' was placed. It is comprised of, and can be divided into, the same sixteen elements of equal size and shape. These elements, made of wooden panels and hinged together, could be easily folded and reconfigured by hand or other simple devices such as pulleys and ropes. The variations of assembly are numerous. During the seasons from spring through to autumn, the Cube takes on various formations of the sixteen elements, depending upon the use of the created space inside. Some outdoor works, exhibition, meditation and temporary sleeping are some of the functions so far realised. During winter, the Cube stays still; an object without motion.

Axonometric of the 'Cube' indicating possible movements of the elements

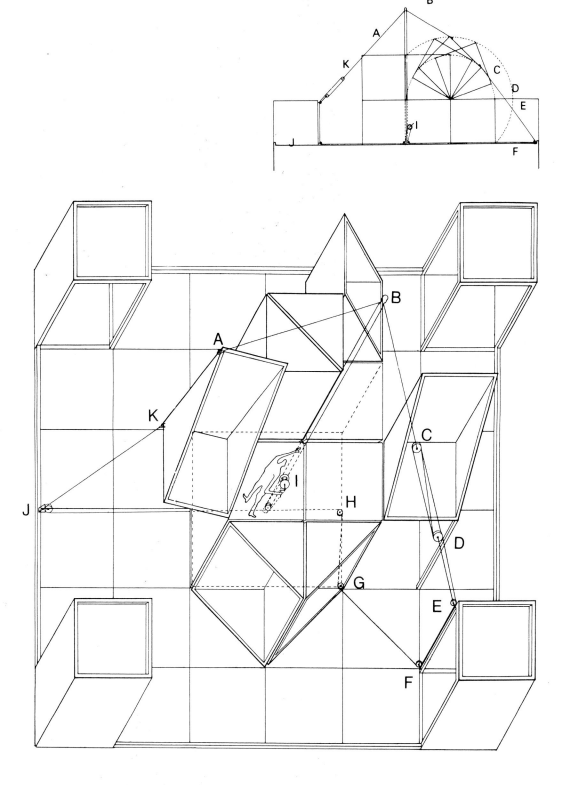

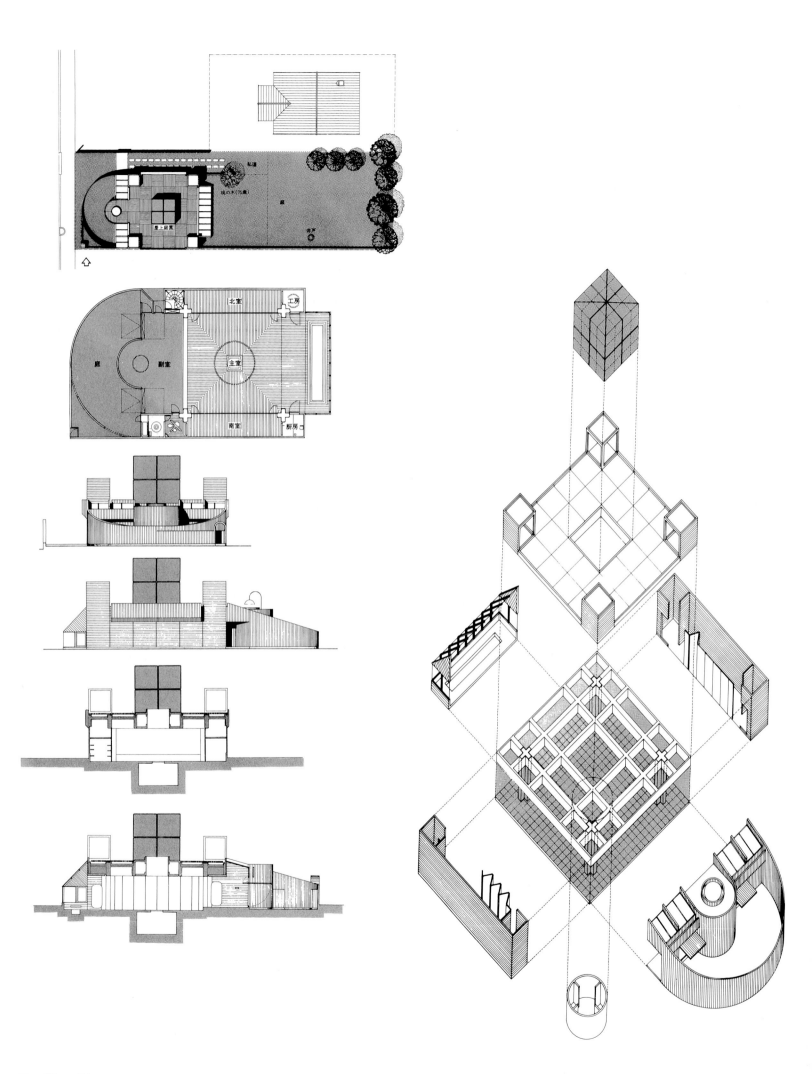

FAR LEFT: *From above, site plan; floor plan; west elevation; north elevation; section; longitudinal section*

LEFT: *Exploded axonometric*

Tokyu 109

Shibuya, Tokyo 1976-78

The building is located in the vicinity of Shibuya station which is one of the busiest downtown areas of Tokyo. As a typical phenomenon of Japanese cities, the area around the station is always crowded with millions of people, who depend on public transportation. Public transport systems are widely and efficiently operated in Japan and a large number of commuters use them in their daily activities.

The triangular site faces directly towards the station and is within easy walking distance from it, on both the street level and underground for subway users. Tokyu Corporation, one of the leading department stores in Shibuya, which also owns a railway system, built this multi-commercial building in order to accommodate boutiques, small stores, restaurants, coffee stores and a small theatre.

After evaluating the streetscape and the urban context in the area, the main direction of the design was focused on the external expression, rather than the interior designs which were carried out by each individual tenant. Takeyama proposed a simple architectural statement against the busy environment or, more precisely, he wanted the building to 'keep its mouth shut and be silent', while all other buildings in the vicinity were brandishing commercial messages. Thus, unlike his previous projects the Ichiban-kan and Niban-kan in Shinjuku, the cylinder and solid rectangular volume of the building appear as plain walls without any special surface pattern.

The cylindrical shaft covered simply with aluminium sheets has become a landmark in the urban district of Shibuya. The cylinder contains two elevators and a stairway and is an extension of the public streets; it connects the street level with the subway concourse below and the roof garden with an open air stage above, somewhat like the twin shafts in Ichiban-kan.

The commission was shared with Tomohiko Komada, architect, whose firm was in charge of working drawings and site supervision.

Elevation

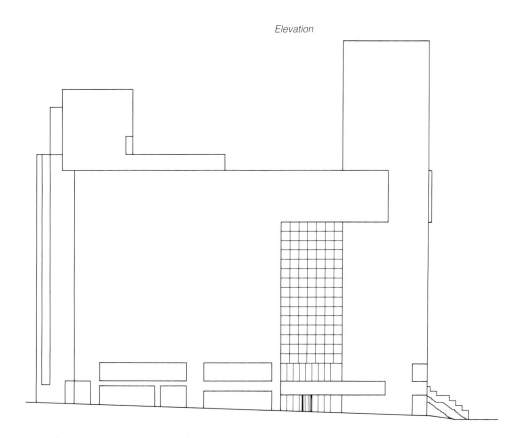

Nakamura Memorial Hospital

Sapporo, Hokkaido 1978–80

The project is a neuro-surgical hospital with 800 beds, located in the middle of Sapporo, the capital of Hokkaido. It is situated in the central medical district of the city.

The design of the hospital consists of three parts: the tall thirteen-storey building which houses the patients' zone, including wards and outpatients area; the low part which is the doctors' zone containing doctors' offices, operation rooms and examination areas; and the main connecting zone in the centre which links four different levels. Four elevators are installed for patients' circulation in the tallest building.

The top floor with its curving roofs is used as a roof garden, greenhouse and solar collecting device, and is open to patients and their attendants. The lower building is five storeys high and accommodates mainly doctors' activities. On the top floor of this building, the dining hall and lounge for nurses also features a vaulted glass roof.

The central connection in between the two main blocks is covered again with a glass roof; this is where corridors form bridges to a lounge encircled by a gallery, where art exhibitions and concerts are periodically held. The external walls are covered with white mosaic tiles of various surface treatments (glossy, matt, embossed) in order to delicately reflect the sunlight in this northern latitude and to give comfort to the patients. The shapes of roofs and the silhouette of the end walls are of circular and metaphorical design, creating an identifiable landmark in the cityscape.

Section through the three parts of the building; the doctors' zone, circulation zone and patients' zone

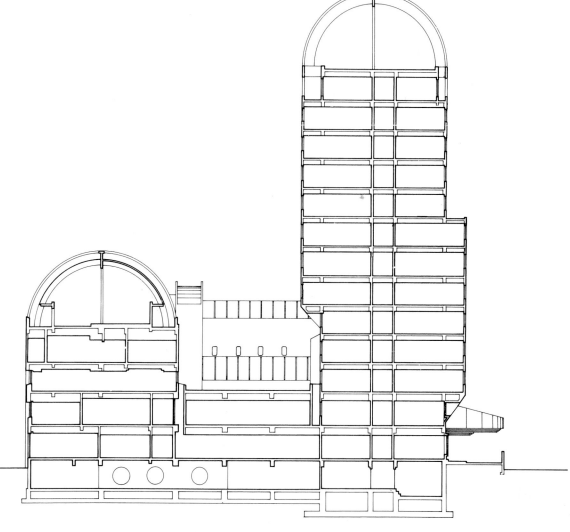

Building No 10, Musashino Art University

Kodaira, Tokyo 1979–81

Building No 10 at the Musashino Art University was planned for three design departments: graphic, stage and basic design. The site is next to the entrance mall to the administration building and faces the central square of the whole campus, which opens towards the surrounding community. In response to this site condition, an identical building form was proposed at the initial stage of design. However, the design solution was required to appear as an extension to Building No 9 in volume and structural framework, following the basic context of the overall campus design.

Since the university dictated that the external expression was to have syntactic continuity with the neighbouring building by utilising a similar structural system and circulation pattern, the existing precedent was matched primarily in internal space design. The area between the double corridors is an atrium connecting the second to fourth floors, and partially down to the first floor. The second floor is the main floor allowing studios and ateliers on the first floor to have high ceilings. The external design was also required to be similar to the adjacent structure, except in the design of windows and details.

Students are permitted to use the entire complex as they wish, with access to the various tools and machinery installed in different parts of the building.

The design commission was shared with Hideo Terada who also teaches at Musashino.

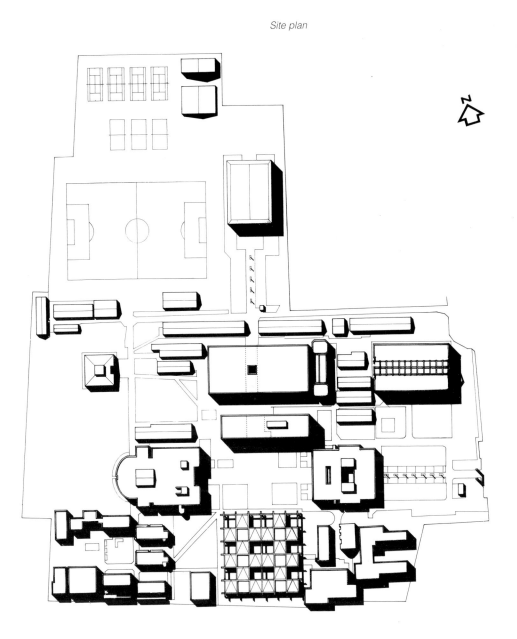

Site plan

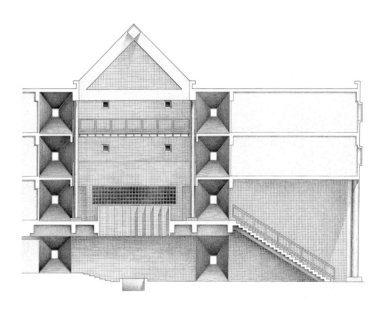

CENTRE: *Rendered section*

Mikakuto Sweet Factory
Yamato-Koriyama, Nara 1984

The programme called for the extension of the existing factory that produces sweets, such as candies, chocolate bars, snacks and Japanese 'gumi'. The old facilities were to be increased fourfold, although the types, system and the capacity of the new production lines were not decided at the outset of the design.

The rectangular site is within a newly developed industrial area in Nara, the first permanent capital (710–794AD) and one of the oldest cities in Japan. The building faces a national road which runs through numerous historical sites and places of interest with well-preserved monuments.

The new extension is a four-storey concrete building placed parallel to the existing structure with an open space in-between. This space is covered with a steel-frame roof and functions as the service area for shipping and receiving, and other activities. The inclined space frame over the courtyard between the new building and the existing factory defines the spaces clearly, and was also conceived as a way to bring continuity to potential extensions which may be built in the future.

The open space in front acts as a buffer zone between the new building and the main road. This area is now a 'story-telling place'. With the facade of the building as the backdrop to this 'stage', dolls and figures made by local artists, depicting characters of the same fairy-tale, have been collected here with the intention to create a 'fairy-tale park'.

In the 'Sweet Factory' design, the primary intention was not to expose the production activities to the outside; instead, the industrial atmosphere was wrapped in a 'sugar coating'. The main reason for this was the environmental context of this rich historical area.

Site plan

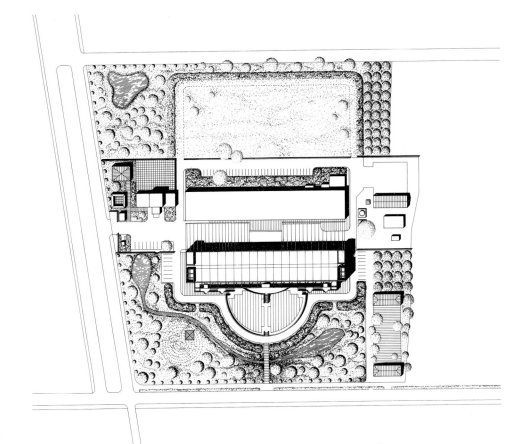

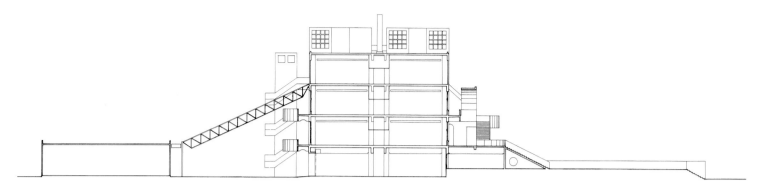

ABOVE: *Section through the building showing (from L to R) original factory, covered service yard, production spaces and garden*

OPPOSITE: *Schematic axonometric*

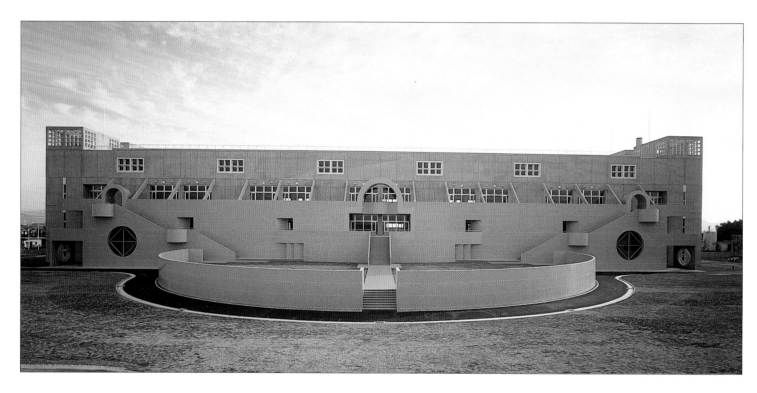

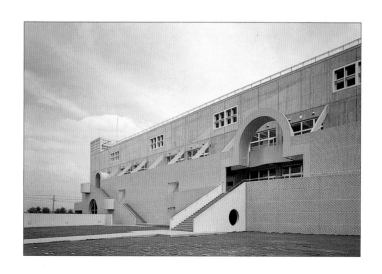

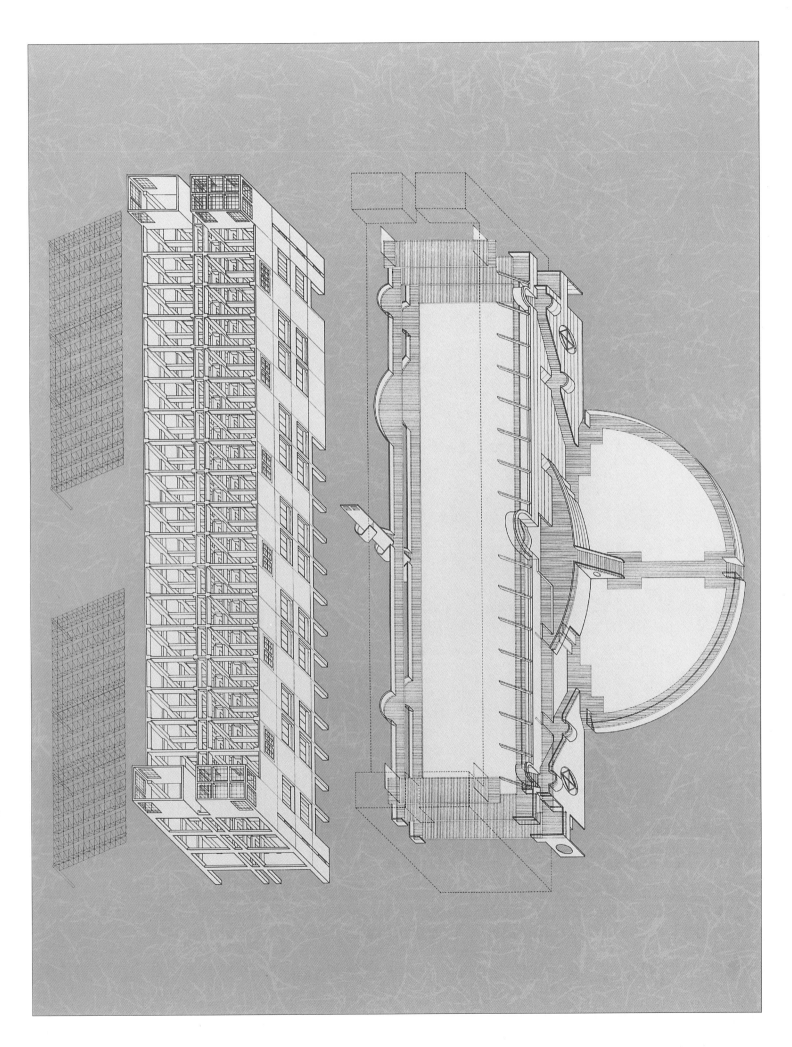

Kyoto Renaissance

Kyoto 1983–86

This is a multiple-use complex including several restaurants, a multi-purpose auditorium, swimming pool, seminar rooms, lecture halls, and workshops for adult education. The triangular site is located in front of the central Kyoto Station. Regulations, such as building codes, fire regulations, and scenic codes, are extremely severe in this traditional city.

Kyoto, at 1,200 years old, is one of the oldest cities and it is the symbol of the traditional cultural heritage of Japan. On the other hand, leading industries in this city are related to advanced technology such as biotechnology, new ceramics, computer industries amongst others. The design goal was to make an architectural statement which utilised the dichotomy of traditional background and progressive content.

The functions of the building are divided three ways: classrooms with a swimming pool and athletics halls on the upper floors; restaurants of diverse cuisines on the lower floors; and a theatre of 200 seats in between, on the fourth floor. In order to accommodate different volumes with various functions which would permit future change-ability, structural framework was proposed that would have left the middle parts of the building as free as possible from columns, by having three major vertical supports at the three corners of the triangular site. This solution, however, was not permitted by the local government, simply because the corner supports would be too vertical externally in contrast to the horizontality of Kyoto's cityscape.

Since the texture and the external finish were strictly controlled, materials used were selected to harmonise with the surroundings. For example, the granite wall is very similar in colour to the roof tiles of existing town houses, while the aluminium framework within the external wall is the same colour as the Golden Pagoda, a national treasury. The overall architectural expression was based on juxtaposing the syntax of masonry and timber framework; in other words, the materials of heavy granite and light aluminium were intended to signify the duality of context this building was destined to have.

Worm's eye axonometric

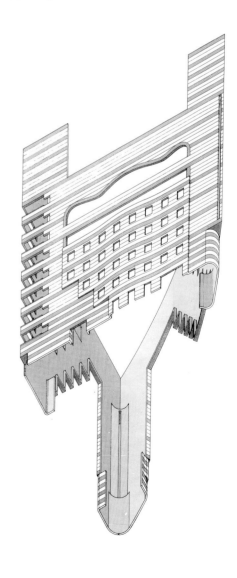

in elevation. All of this is held together by a grey, charcoal, and black granite envelope whose banding differentiates base, shaft, and cap. The result makes coherent a blend of diverse elements that is sometimes surprising, especially when the southeast corner comes into view on approach from the nearby back streets.

The metal screen, a glass curtain wall, and a sandstone wall with classically detailed windows mark the transition of the double-height ground floor from the Japanese centre of culture without to its European counterpart within. Located midway in this passage, the lobby stair combines modern materials and a trompe l'œil concept which originated with the fifteenth century's 'discovery' of perspective. By leading the visitor in, up, and seemingly back outside through the large landing window, the stair represents the carefully studied interdependence that is at the heart of Takeyama's Renaissance.

Michael Green, 'Renaissance-KYOTO', *A+U*, November 1986 (used here with permission)

Michael Green commented the following on the Renaissance:

First impressions of acute-angled corners, extended service towers, and shallow curves raise the question of whether or not Renaissance is more than just another building-as-ship metaphor. Closer inspection, however, reveals an exterior in which stepped frameworks, bowed walls, and punched openings cleverly vie with each other for supremacy across adjacent facades. On the entrance side the entire structure's curved sweep edges out a six storey frame for primary importance while on the south, stepping predominates.

For the east wall Takeyama used the punched openings to disguise a stack of fire escape corridors and turns the bowed balcony plan into a giant teahouse window

OPPOSITE RIGHT: *Exploded axonometric*

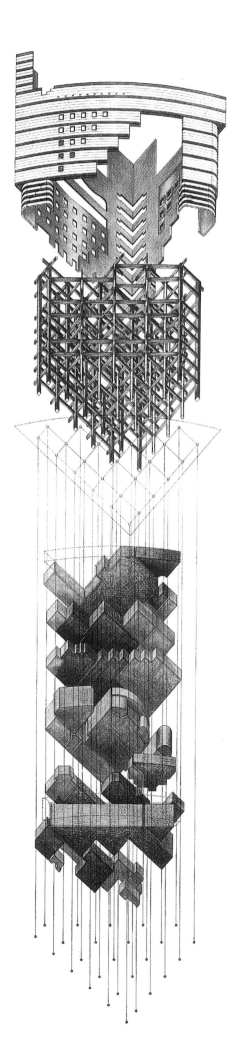

Egyptian Embassy

Tokyo 1984–86

The main functional areas of this building are a chancellery, reception halls, and the ambassador's residence. The narrow site, which steps down towards the south, is located in the middle of Tokyo. At two different levels the site connects to two adjacent streets: a main street in the north and a sloping back street on the south-western end, which also represent two urban zones; the front commercial and the back residential.

Within the six-level building, reception halls and ambassador's residence are on the upper floors with a formal entrance from the main street and the offices of the chancellery are on the lower three floors with a rather informal access from the back street. The maximum use of the given site, and the effective application of the local building regulations, did not leave sufficient open space and so Takeyama created roof gardens at each office floor which cascade down from the fourth floor to the basement.

The design aim was to create an architectural entity of exemplary quality that would serve as a focus for the surrounding environment. Both for the internal space organisation and the external expression, a duality of 'formality' and 'informality' was implemented. These two qualities were not necessarily expressed in an explicit manner but were merged into an ambiguous entity.

There is no literal architectural expression on the facade that signifies national identity. Instead, the national flag was considered to be a sufficiently powerful symbol of Egypt; the building itself was treated as the 'platform' for raising the flag. This was mainly due to the surrounding urban context, especially along the main street,

which is already heavily commercialised and crowded with multiple signs. With the national flag on the top of the building, a certain formality for both the main entrance area (including the pilotis) and the entry to the ambassador's residence was carefully preserved.

Site plan

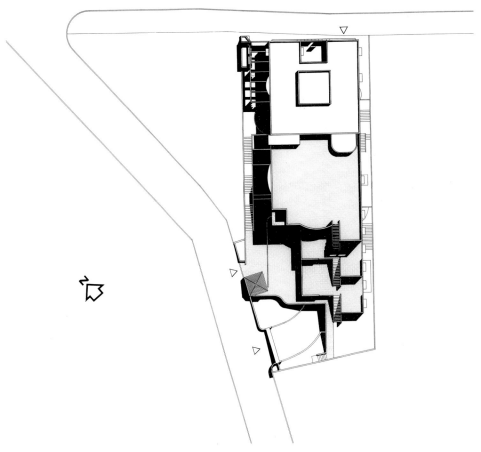

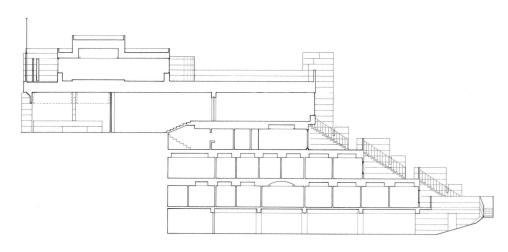

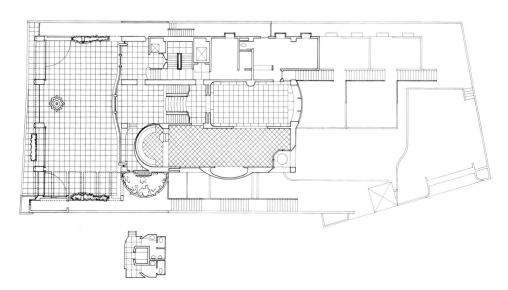

ABOVE RIGHT: *Section through building from upper street level to the lower street level at the rear*

CENTRE: *Third floor plan (upper street level), showing the ambassador's residence*

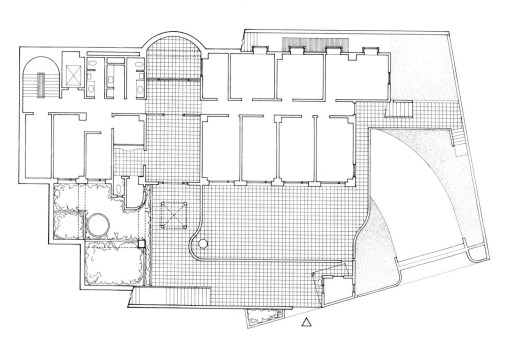

ABOVE: *Southwest elevation*

OPPOSITE BELOW: *Ground floor
plan (lower street level showing the
offices*

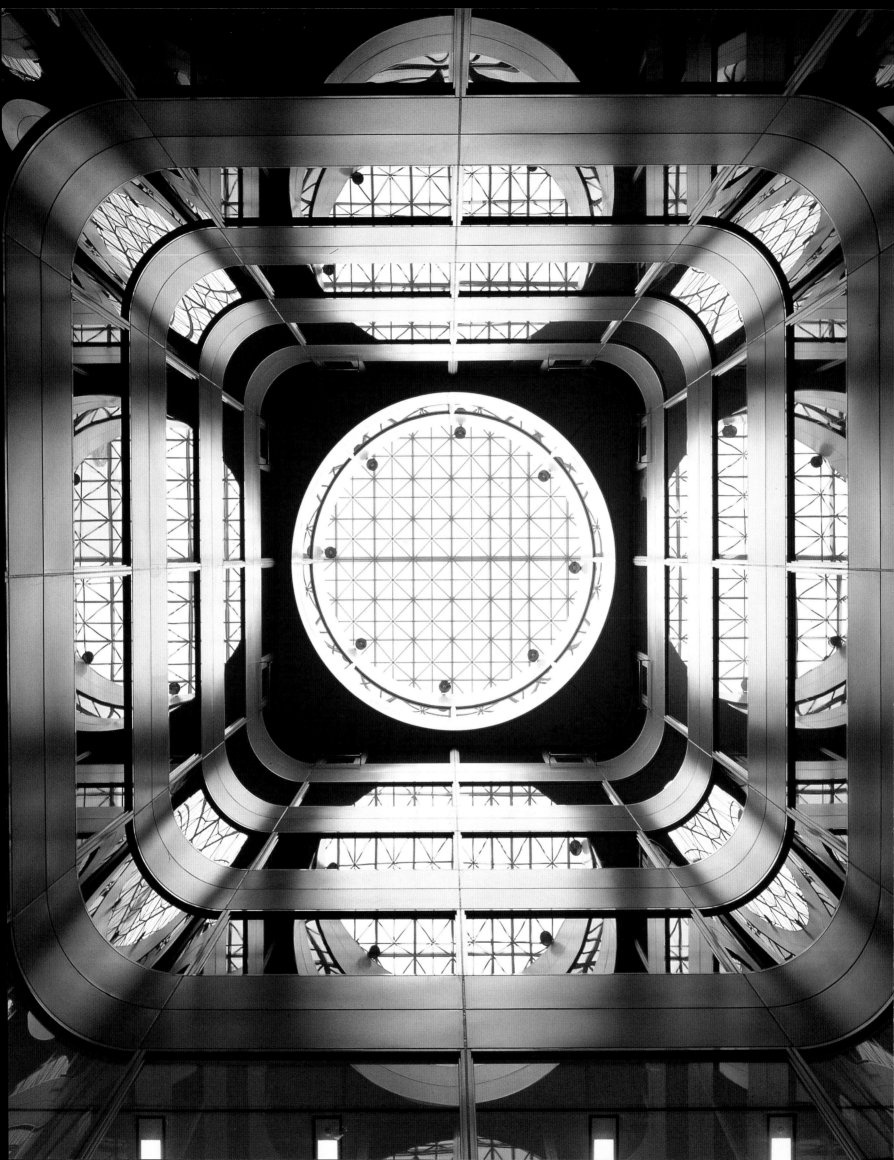

Five Office Towers

Position Building, Shinjuku Tokyo 1988–90

Canal Tower, Nihonbashi Tokyo 1988–91

Neoage Nakameguro, Meguro Tokyo 1989–90

Tech Hiroo, Meguro Tokyo 1990–92

Mikakuto, Osaka 1990–92

Land ownership in Japanese urban districts is a grey area full of uncertainties due to many long traditions and the lack of a clear land policy. One of the most peculiar aspects of the situation is the pattern of sub-division, which, although it can be topological, reveals an increasing fragmentation with ever smaller and more irregularly shaped lots, even along major urban streets.

Moreover, between buildings along the same main streets narrow spaces are left open and unused. These unused gaps can add up to as much as an average of five per cent of the total length of densely built streets. The gaps, mainly the result of civil law rather than building codes, exist to lessen conflicts among neighbours or property owners by establishing a series of 'twilight zones' between them.

These structural developments, alongside economic reasons and land ownership, have created the extremely uneven streetscape and heterogeneous frontage in Japanese cities.

The five Office Towers are not located in the same urban area, but share a disposition of site. Being called locally 'pencil building[s]', these towers function as rental offices, accommodating 100 to 300 square metres of rental space plus toilets and kitchenettes on each floor. The buildings have been named by their respective owners for various reasons.

OPPOSITE: *Mikakuto*

BELOW: *Mikakuto; section through atrium*

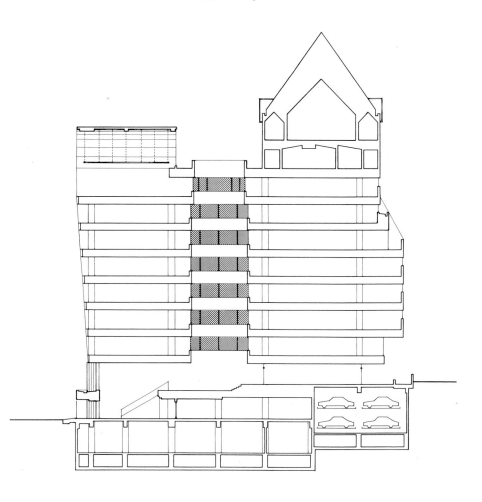

OPPOSITE ABOVE: *Entrance to Canal Tower*

OPPOSITE BELOW LEFT: *Entrance approach to Tech Hiroo*

OPPOSITE BELOW RIGHT: *Position Building*

ABOVE L to R: *Elevations of Mikakuto, front and rear facades; Neoage Nakameguro*

BELOW L to R: *Elevations of Position Building; Canal Tower, front and rear facades*

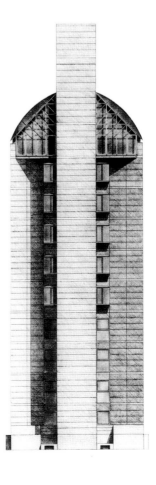

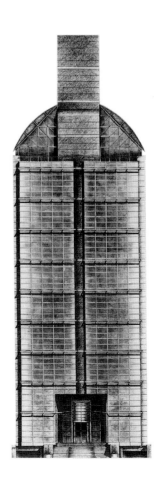

Tech Hiroo

Position Building

Canal Tower

Mikakuto

Neoage Nakameguro

Tokyo Port Terminal

Harumi, Tokyo 1991

This Passenger Terminal serves the principal purposes of international travel. The two major activities are: the essential functions, such as administration, immigration and passport control, customs inspection, luggage handling, reception, arrival and departure; and the public service functions, such as event hall, gallery, restaurant, observation deck and plazas. The building was planned and built in commemoration of the fiftieth anniversary of the establishment of the International Port of Tokyo.

The Terminal is located at the edge of reclaimed land in the harbour, along the waterfront of Tokyo Bay, and forms a symbolic gate between the water and the city. The design intended to convey a multiplicity of messages through a single architectural language, signifying among other things, the point of arrival with its feeling of relief that travellers experience after a long voyage and, for the citizens, a point of reference indicating where the land meets with the water.

In the overall syntax, two intersecting axes play dominant roles; one is parallel with the water's edge, and the other is oriented towards the remote views of the still heavily industrialised port and a new suspension bridge which was completed in 1993.

The main facilities are arranged under a platform that rises from the entrance plaza at street level up to the main roof garden, and continues down to the waterfront park south of the terminal. The upper facilities for public services have been designed as an airy composition, with solids and voids. Its house-like quality is expressed by the steel-frame pyramid, which creates a single powerful landmark; for travellers against the unstable cityscape, and for downtowners against the industrial vernacular that surrounds them in the port area. The four membranous domes over the observation deck are lit from the inside after dark.

Exploded axonometric

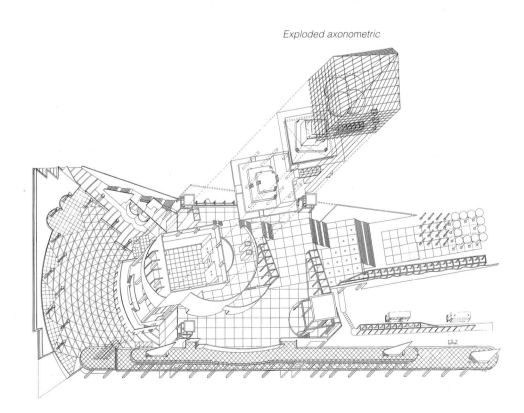

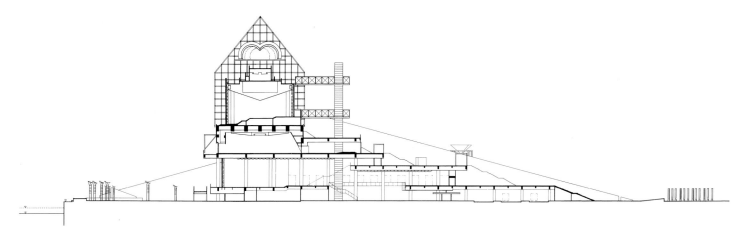

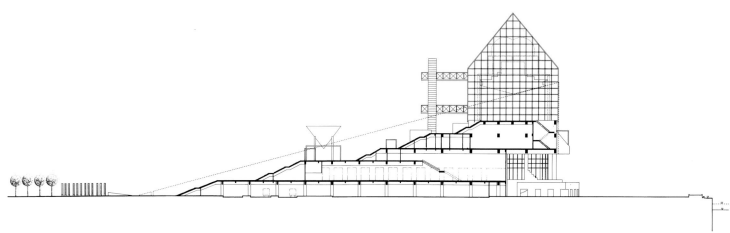

ABOVE: *Sections through the Port Terminal; through the main passenger areas, above, and through the garages, below*

OPPOSITE: *Paving layout*

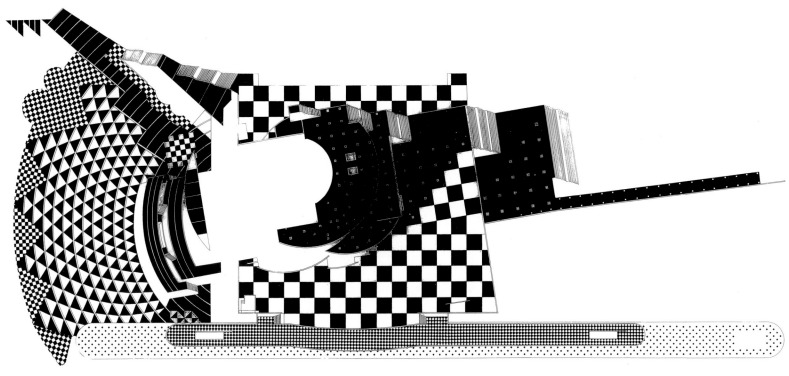

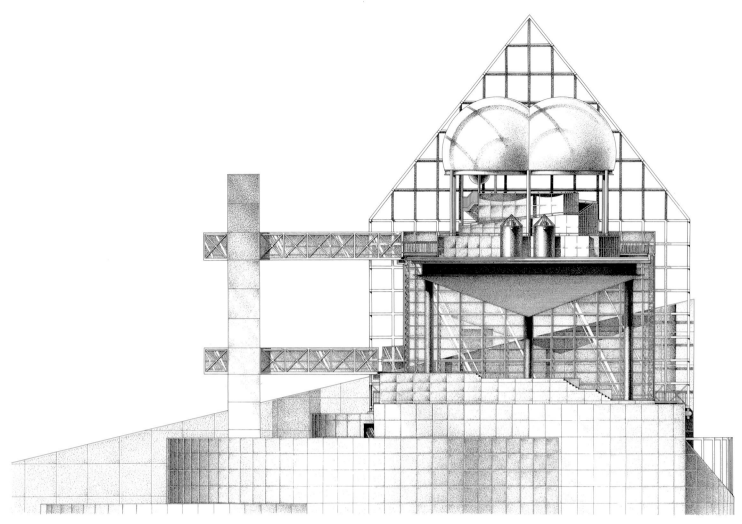

Rendered elevation

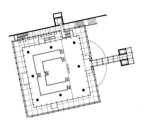

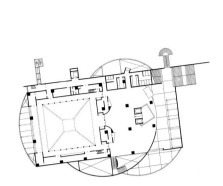

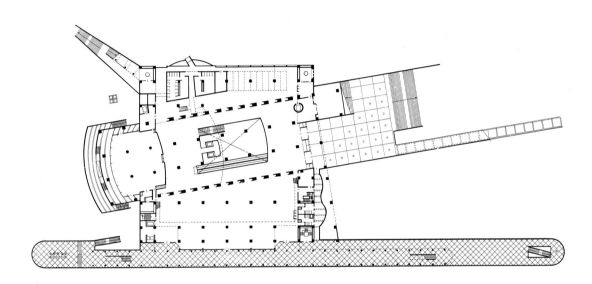

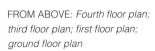

FROM ABOVE: *Fourth floor plan; third floor plan; first floor plan; ground floor plan*

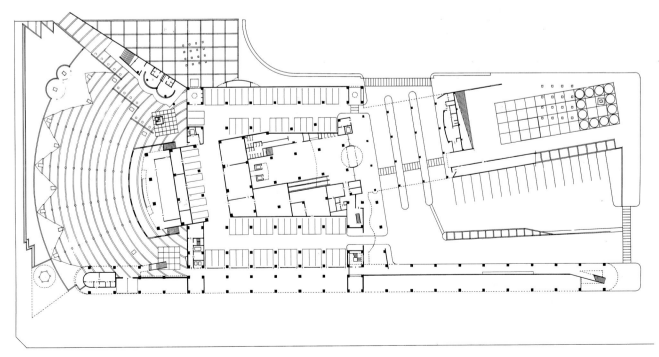

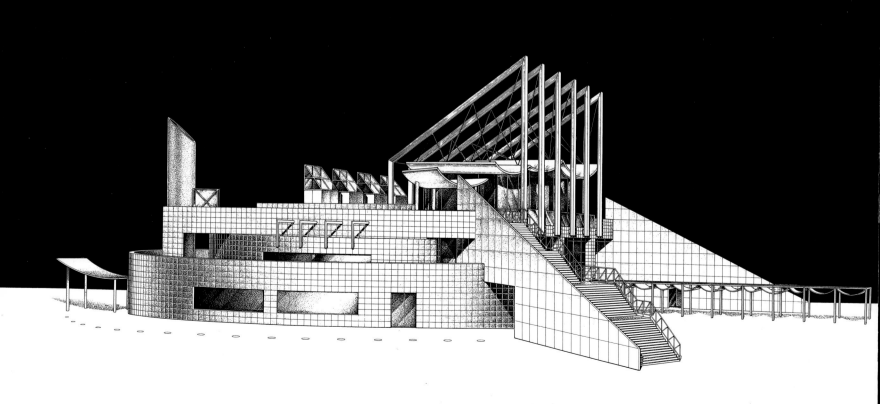

Tokyo Port, Satellite Terminal

Harumi, Tokyo 1995

The Satellite Terminal was planned as a supplementary facility to the main Tokyo Port Terminal which was completed in 1991. In recent years, more than 100 passenger boats from abroad are reported to visit Tokyo Port annually and new pier facilities are needed. Extending the concourse on the eastern edge of the main Terminal, the Satellite was designed with similar functions to the main Terminal, including waiting lobby, passport and custom inspection, luggage claim and visitors' area. Most activities for passengers are accommodated in the Satellite, but for conveniences such as restaurants, shops, etc, passengers have to depend on the main terminal reached either by walking on the concourse or by shuttle bus.

Although the Satellite belongs to the main terminal functionally, it needs its own visual identity for the passengers and visitors. The expression of the relationship of similarity and/or dissimilarity between the two was one of the design goals.

The articulation of the Satellite is similar to the main terminal in some respects, but dissimilar in other aspects. For instance, the open-framed pyramid, one of the dominant features of the main terminal, created a landmark and a seamark. For the Satellite,

although the same transparent effect was kept, the frame is less monumental and oriented to one side in order to 'indicate' the way to the main terminal.

The interior of the Satellite is designed to be homologically different from the main Terminal. While the white-painted lobby of the main Terminal has a large glass wall towards the south where the port bridge has just recently been completed, the lobby and inspection space of the Satellite will be enclosed without having any view out. Also instead of white, it will be coloured with metaphorical graphics and decorations on the enclosing walls.

In the future, two more satellite terminals will be constructed along the waterfront.

OPPOSITE: *Perspective view*

BELOW: *Site plan showing the Main Terminal and the Satellite Terminal*

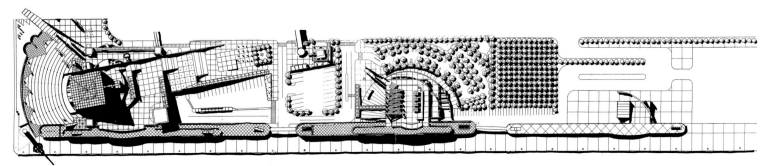

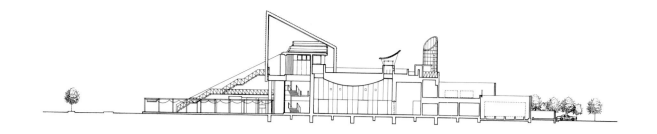

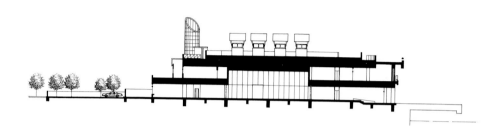

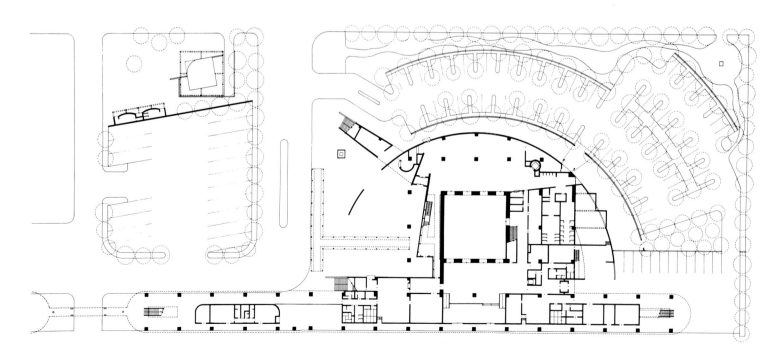

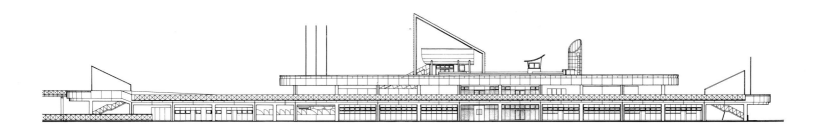

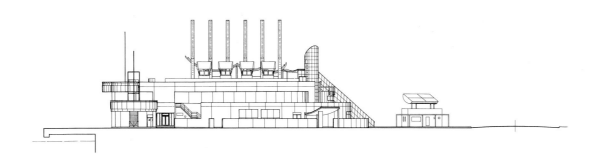

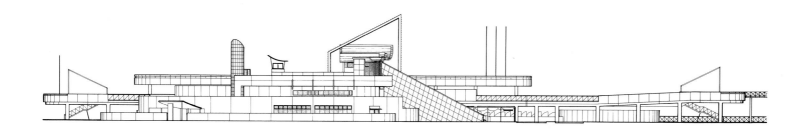

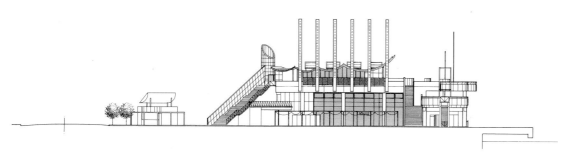

OPPOSITE ABOVE: *Sections through the site*

OPPOSITE BELOW: *Ground plan*

ABOVE: *Elevations*

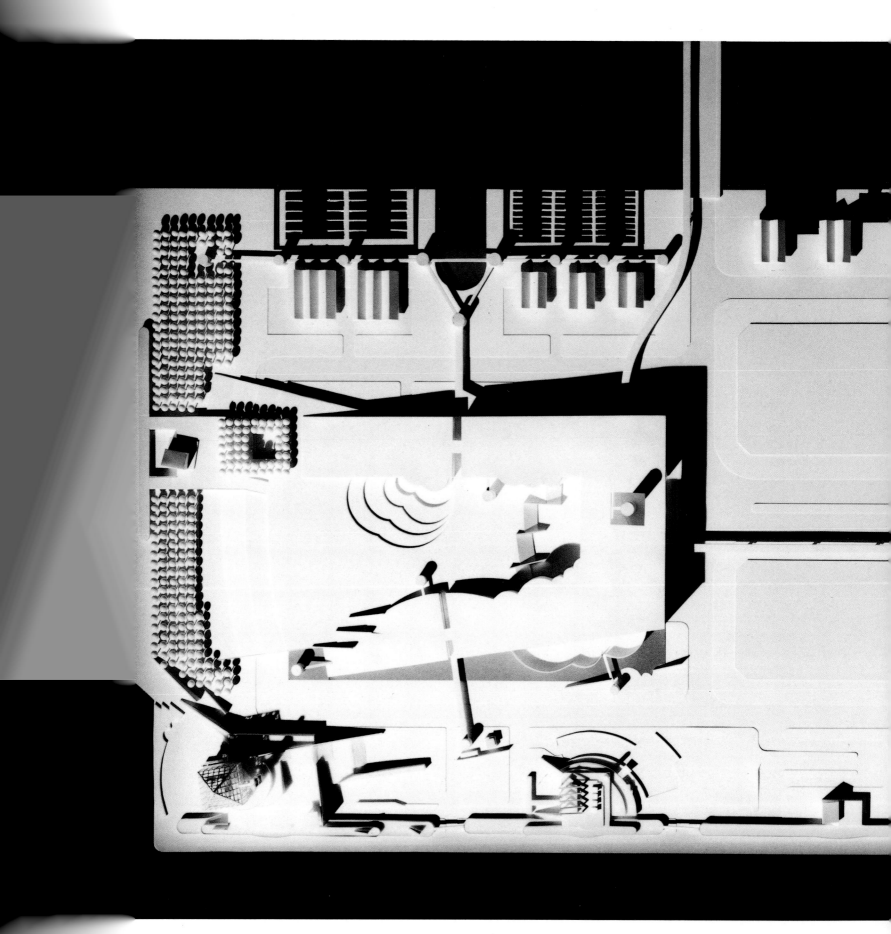

Harumi Island Project

Tokyo 1993

Harumi is a reclaimed island in the Port of Tokyo and is located very close to the city centre. The government owns the majority of the island which at present is a rather bleak environment with mainly industrial sites, warehouses, exhibition halls and some public housing. When the present development plan is completed, which was proposed by the city authorities for other reclaimed islands (for an estimated population of 110,000) located further from the central districts, Harumi Island will become a very important node between the centre of the city and the newly proposed sub-centres. Access to the island, by both boat and new surface transit systems, has been improved and the privately owned properties in the surrounding urban districts are rapidly becoming built up.

Takeyama's proposal will not allow any further construction in this part of the island, preserving the open space as much as possible. The remaining area will become an important city park along the waterfront.

The southwestern end of the island will be covered with greenery and trees on top of a man-made hill. The necessary facilities as planned by the city authorities, such as an exhibition space, marine station, hotel rooms and transportation, will be installed under the 'hill', with provision for daylighting and privacy. The Port Terminal in the south-east corner of the site will have three more satellites and a marina along the edges.

Thus Harumi Island will become one of the few places in Tokyo where citizens can get together freely at any time of the day, observe the entire cityscape and discover the urban identity of the city in its relationship to the sea.

Upper level plan

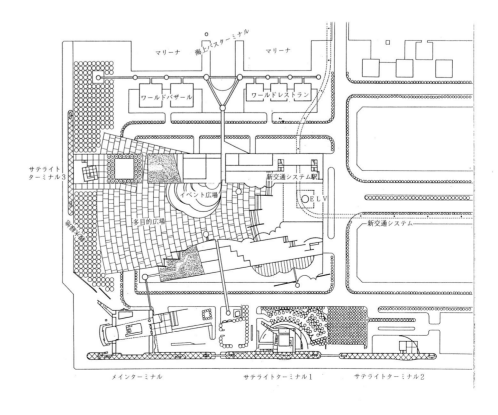

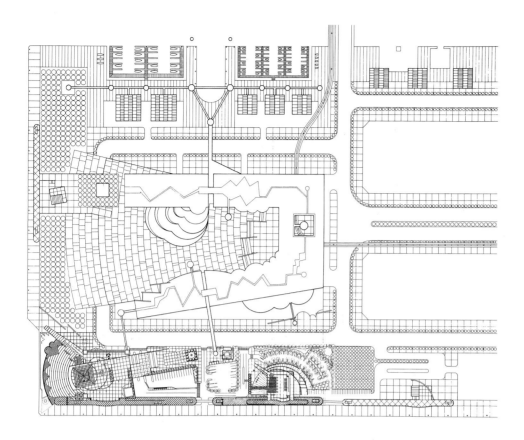

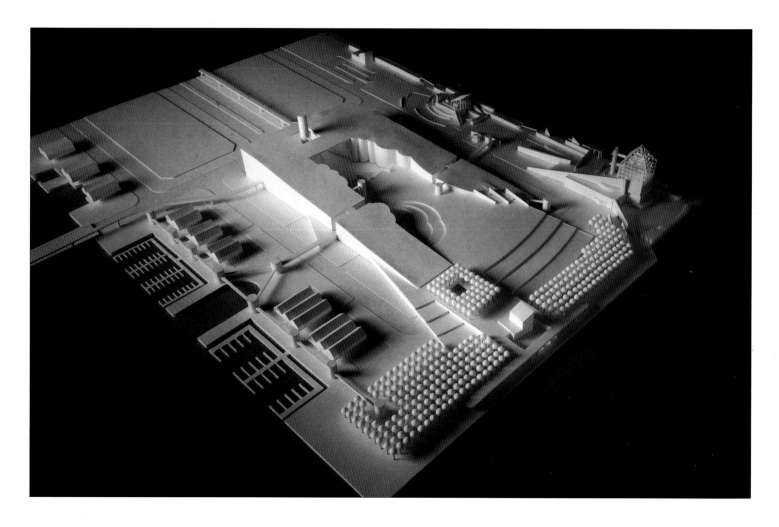

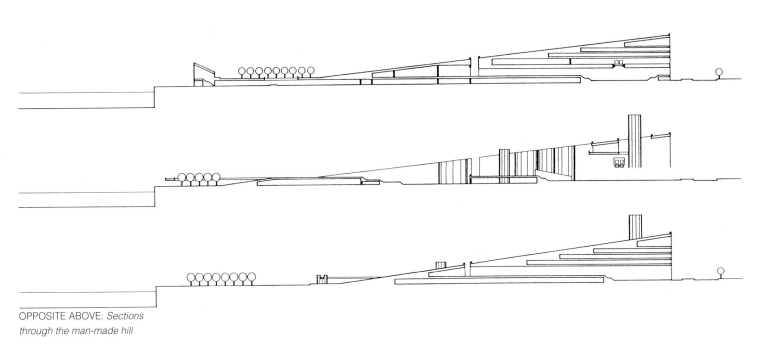

OPPOSITE ABOVE: *Sections through the man-made hill*

OPPOSITE: *Ground level plan*

Nichima Hall

Tonami, Toyama Prefecture 1995

Nichima was one of the leading textile manufacturers in this locality, but recently the business has become more diversified due to the recession in the textile industry.

The site is in the town of Tonami, Toyama Prefecture, where the client established its main industry a few decades ago. Rebuilding the existing unused factory facilities, a hotel has been built using two parallel buildings which were once used as dormitories for factory workers. This alteration job was done by local architects.

The second venture, in which Takeyama is involved, is to convert the old factory building into a multi-purpose hall, named Nichima Hall, in relation to the existing hotel. The new section will accommodate a hall, which can function as an exhibition space, concert and convention hall. In a similar way, the rest of the old facilities will be converted gradually to new functions in the future.

The design solution is based on the intention to reuse as much of the factory building as possible. Therefore, the purpose of the design was to achieve a wholly integrated entity by orchestrating both the old and new component of the project. The 'oxymoron' principle was applied, in which the previous steel building co-exists with the proposed new architecture, allowing visitors to enjoy both past reminiscences and entertain future expectations within the same environment.

Additional design and construction on the site will follow the biulding's completion.

OPPOSITE: *Model of proposed development*

BELOW: *Rendered section*

OVERLEAF: *Rendered elevation*

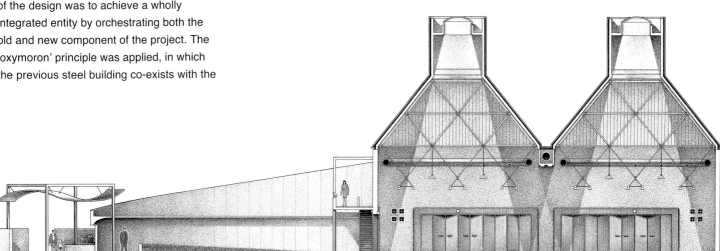

Biography

Minoru Takeyama

Date of Birth
15 March 1934

Place of Birth
Sapporo, Japan

Education

1960	Master Degree, Graduate School of Design, Harvard University
1958	Master Degree, Graduate School of Architecture, Waseda University
1956	Bachelor Degree, School of Architecture, Waseda University

Position

1965–	Principal of Minoru Takeyama & U/A
1975–	Professor at the School of Architecture, Musashino Art University, Tokyo

Membership

AIA	American Institute of Architects (Honourable Fellow)
AIJ	Architectural Institute of Japan
JIA	Japan Institute of Architects

Prizes and Awards

Academic

1990	Plym Distinguished Professorship, University of Illinois Urbana-Champaign
1975	Fulbright Research Fellowship, Massachusetts Institute of Technology and University of California, Berkeley
1973	Wheelwright Fellowship, from Harvard University
1959	Fulbright Grant, (Graduate Student), at Harvard University
1956–58	OKUMA Fellowship of Waseda University
1956	Togo Murano Prize of Waseda University

Professional

1993	Honourable Award, Waterfront Design, USA for Tokyo Port Terminal
1993	Tokyo Design Award, The Best Design Award for Tokyo Port Terminal
1992	International Illumination Design Award for Tokyo Port Terminal (Illumination Engineering Society of North America)
1992	Tokyo Architectural Award for Tokyo Port Terminal (Architectural Office Association, Tokyo)
1992	JCD Annual Design Award for Tokyo Port Terminal
1987	Annual Design Award, Osaka Architects Association
1982	Award, International Design Competition for the State Mosque in Baghdad, Iraq
1981	Second Prize in the International Urban Design Competition for Abu Nuwaz Conservation Project, Baghdad, Iraq
1981	Special Prize (Bronze Medal) in the First World Biennial of Architecture, Bulgaria
1980	Honourable Mention in the International Design Competition for Islamic Cultural Center, Madrid
1975	Silver Medal of JDDA (Japan Display Design Association)
1974	JCD Annual Design Award for Hotel Beverly Tom
1974	Annual Prize of Commercial Design Association
1973	Annual Award of CDA for Rotiny
1971	JCD Annual Design Award for Ichiban-kan
1957	Grand Prize in San Paulo Biennial, (collaboration)

Teaching

Overseas only

1989–90	Plym Distinguished Professor, University of Illinois Urbana-Champaign
1987	Visiting Professor, Harvard University, spring semester
1986,	
1977–79	Visiting Professor, University of California, Berkeley, spring semesters
1985	Lecturer, INVIRON, Singapore, January
1984	Visitor, 'AIR Architecture International, Rotterdam', Rotterdam, May
1984	Panellist, NEO CON, Chicago, May
1983	Visiting Professor, National University of Singapore
1981	Visiting Professor, University of Hong Kong
1979	Visiting Critic, University of Manitoba, Winnipeg
1978	A New Wave of Japanese Architecture, (ten lectures in ten cities), IAUS
1962–63	Teacher, Royal Danish Academy of Fine Arts, Copenhagen, Denmark

Exhibitions

1993	'Retrospective', Tokyo Designers Space, February
1989–90	'Work of Minoru Takeyama', University of Illinois; Kansas State University, USA
1987	'Contemporary Japanese Architecture', (travelling)
1987	'Architecture of Imagination', San Diego State University
1986	'Vision Der Moderne', DAM (Deutsches Architekturmuseum), West Germany
1985	'50 Outstanding Architects of the World', Belgrade Triennial
1985	'Venice Project', (Accademia Bridge), Biennial
1984	'Japan AIR', Central Library, Rotterdam
1981	'Post-Modern Architecture', Louisiana Museum, Copenhagen
1981	'Terra-2', Wroclaw, Poland
1981	'The First World Biennial of Architecture', Sophia, Bulgaria
1981	'Recent Work', University of Hong Kong
1978	'A New Wave of Japanese Architecture', (IAUS, New York), ten cities in the USA

Chronological List of Work: 1965–99

1965 Restaurant Savarin, interior design, Ginza, Tokyo
Restaurant Pandora, interior design, Akasaka, Tokyo, 1965–66

1966 Takeyama House, Sapporo, unbuilt
National Theater, Tokyo, competition
Low-rise housing, Copenhagen, Denmark, competition

1967 Espoo Project, Finland, competition

1968 Kinichi-kan Department Store, Sapporo, Hokkaido, unbuilt
Nagano Young Men's House, lodge, Nagano, 1968–69
Memorial for the War Dead, monument, Otaru, Hokkaido, 1968–69
Ichiban-kan, commercial complex, Shinjuku, Tokyo, 1968–69
Niban-kan, commercial complex, Shinjuku, Tokyo, 1968–70
Shigeyama House, Suginami, Tokyo, 1968–70
Boutique Mammina, interior design, Tokyo, 1968–70
Katsura House, Setagaya, Tokyo, 1968–69
Showroom, interior design, Tokyo, 1968–70
Amsterdam City Hall, Amsterdam, Holland, competition
Wien Conference Center, Wien, Austria, competition

1969 Utonai Lakeshore Center, commercial complex, Hokkaido, 1969–70
Labor Union Hall, auditorium and offices, Omiya, Saitama, 1969–70
Tea House 'TOPS', interior design, Nihonbashi, Tokyo, 1969–70

1970 Iwakura Office, Tomakomai, Hokkaido, 1970–71
World Experimental College, Thy, Denmark, unbuilt
Shimada House, Azabu, Tokyo, 1970–71
Betto House, Azabu, Tokyo, 1970–71
'Body Furniture', items of furniture
Shu-Pub, interior design, three shoe stores in Tokyo, 1970–80

1971 Gas Station and Drive-in Restaurant, Mikasa, Hokkaido, 1971–72
Pepsi-Cola Bottling Plant, factory building, Mikasa, Hokkaido, 1971–72
Plateau (Pompidou Centre competition), Paris

1972 Hotel Beverly Tom, Tomakomai City, Hokkaido, 1972–73
Restaurant 'Sanbi', Los Angeles
Iwakura House, Tomakomai City, Hokkaido, 1972–73

1973 High-density Low-rise Housing, housing project, Tomakomai, Hokkaido
Iwamoto House, Sapporo, Hokkaido, 1973–74

Parlor Yamagiwa, interior design, Akihabara, Tokyo, 1973–74

1974 Misawa Showroom, interior design, Takaido, Tokyo
Living Environment of Northern Regions, exhibition design, Sapporo, Hokkaido

1975 Shell Garden, gas station, Roppongi, Tokyo
Atelier Indigo, architect's own studio, Sapporo, Hokkaido, 1975–76
Yoshimura House, Sapporo, Hokkaido, 1975–76
Ukon House, Suginami, Tokyo, 1975–76
Porto Santos Island Project, Porto Santos, competition

1976 Sapporo Art Park, Sapporo, Hokkaido, project

1977 Tokyu Store '109', commercial complex, Shibuya, Tokyo, 1977–78
Hakozaki House, Fukushima
Kunimatsu House, Sapporo, Hokkaido, 1977–78

1978 Restaurant Pops, Kusakabe, Saitama
Nakamura Mountain House, Niseko, Hokkaido, 1978–79
Ogyu House, Niseko, Hokkaido, 1978–79

1979 Harajuku House, condominium, Harajuku, Tokyo, 1979–80
Nakamura Memorial Hospital, Sapporo, Hokkaido, 1979–80
Kawamura House, Sapporo, Hokkaido, 1979–80
Nishinomiya House, Kawasaki, 1979–80
Islamic Cultural Centre, Madrid, competition

1980 Building No 10, Musashino Art University, Kodaira, Tokyo, 1980–81
Art Building, Musashino Art University, Kodaira, Tokyo, 1980–81
Kanai House, Toshima-ku, Tokyo, 1980–81
Itabashi House, Sapporo, 1980–82
Cafe Porta, interior design, Yokohama, 1980–81

1981 Car Shop Seibu, Kabe, Saitama, 1981–82
Arai House, Sapporo, 1981–82
Nakamura House, Sapporo, 1981–82
Abu Nuwaz Redevelopment Project, Baghdad, Iraq, urban design competition
Arab International Conference Hall, USE, invited competition

1982 Twin Towers, Mexico, Mexico City, unbuilt hotel and office
State Mosque, Baghdad, invited competition

1983 Mikakuto 'Sweet' Factory, Yamato-Koriyama, Nara, 1983–84

1985 'Renaissance', commercial complex, Kyoto, 1985–86
Egyptian Embassy, Meguro, Tokyo, 1985–86
Hashi House, Sapporo, 1985–86
Hattori House, Suginami, Tokyo, 1985–86

Hash Puppie, interior design, Shibuya, Tokyo
'Accademia Bridge, Venice Project', Venice, proposal for the Biennale

1986 Hayashibara House, Okayama, 1986–87

1987 Kitami Hokuto Hospital, Kitami, Hokkaido, 1987–88
Oasa General Hospital, Ebetsu, Hokkaido, unbuilt
Mishima House, Otaru, Hokkaido, 1987–88
Volcano Maruyama, interior design, Sapporo, Hokkaido, 1987–88
Aichi Cultural Center, Nagoya, competition

1988 'Position' Building, office tower, Shinjuku, Tokyo, 1988–90
Canal Tower, office tower, Nihonbashi, Tokyo, 1988–91
Tokyo Port Terminal, passenger terminal, Harumi, Tokyo, 1988–91

1989 Neoage Nakameguro, office tower, Meguro, Tokyo, 1989–90
Life Avenue, apartment house, Otaru, Hokkaido, 1989–90
Azabu Clinic, interior design, Sapporo, Hokkaido, 1989–90
Ibusuki Redevelopment Project, Kago-shima, urban planning

1990 Alpenrose, resort hotel, Kusatsu (hot spring), Gunma, 1990–92
Hiroo Tech, office tower, Shibuya, Tokyo, 1990–92
Volcano Himeji, interior design, Himeji, Hyogo
Mikakuto Tower, offices, Osaka, 1990–92

1991 Meguro Office Building, Meguro, Tokyo, 1991–92
Sapporo Factory, commercial complex, Sapporo, Hokkaido, 1991–93
Takahashi House, Sapporo, Hokkaido, 1991–92
Grandiose Yamate, condominium, Yoko-hama, 1991–92

1992 Terme International Hotel, Sapporo, Hokkaido, 1992–93
Restaurant Mortier, interior design, Hiroo, Tokyo, 1992–93

1993 Spreebogen Project, Berlin, Germany, urban design competition

1994 Tokyo Port Satellite Terminal, passenger terminal, Harumi, Tokyo, not yet built
Nichima Hall, convention centre, Tonami, Toyama, to be built by 1995
Central Station, Dalian, Dalian, project
Yokohama Port Terminal, Yokohama, open competition

1995 Shinjuku Underground Passage, urban corridors, Shinjuku, Tokyo, to be built by 1999

1996 Yokohama North Crematorium, Yokohama, to be built by 1999

Bibliography

Publications by Minoru Takeyama

Periodicals

'Space Situation', *Kindai Kenchiku*, May 1968

'Space Relation', *Kenchiku*, September 1968

'Space Situationing', *Toshi Jutaku*, March 1969

'Membrane', *Kenchiku*, July 1970

'Membrane', *Shinkenchiku*, July 1970

'Territoriality', *Space Design*, August 1970

'On Arne Jacobsen', *Kenchikuka*, Autumn 1970; and *Architecture + Urbanism*, October 1971

'Hvor for eller Hvor for ikke, Expo?' (Danish), *Arckitekten*, No. 9 1970

'On Robert Venturi', *A+U*, October 1971

'On Architectural Education', *Public Architecture*, May 1972

'Architecture and Fashion', *Kenchiku Zasshi* (Architectural Institute of Japan Journal), July 1972

'Counter-Architecture 1', *Kenchiku Bunka*, August 1973

'Architecture and Languages', *Space Design*, January 1973

'Revision of Internationalism', *A+U*, May 1973

'Pedagogical Architecture', *A+U*, October 1973

'Counter-Architecture 2', *Kenchiku Bunka*, January 1974

'Imago-encephalogram', *Space Design*, January 1974

'Grouping and Collection', *Kenchiku Bunka*, August 1974

'New Dimension of Architectural Education', *Kenchiku Zasshi (AIJ Journal)*, October 1974

'Street Semiology', (guest editor to whole issue), *Kenchiku Bunka*, February 1975

'Ideation and Technology', (English), *UIA Journal*, XII 1975

'Contemporary Interior Design', *Japan Interior*, December 1975

'Heterology in Architecture', (English), *The Japan Architect*, June 1976

'From Architecture to Architecture', *Space Design*, November 1976

'Soft Technology', *Shinkenchiku*, September 1976

'Form and Image', *Shinkenchiku*, September 1977

'Multivalence of Architecture', *Kenchiku Bunka*, September 1977

'Modernology', *A+U*, August 1978

'Semantic Approach to Architecture', *Kenchiku Zasshi (AIJ Journal)*, April 1979

'Background of Post-Modernism', *A+U*, October 1979

'Architecture in the 1980s', *A+U*, January 1980

'Role of Architects and Society', *Shinkenchiku*, August 1980

'On Historicism in Architecture', *Kendai Kenchiku*, January 1981

'Interior Landscape', *Kenchiku Bunka*, February 1981

'Form and Function', *Shinkenchiku*, June 1981

'Urban Languages', *Kenchiku Bunka*, June 1981

'Inside and Outside of Time', *Space Design*, February 1982

'Western Classicism in Japan', (English), *Architectural Design* 1/2 1982

'Japan's Architectural Schizophrenia', (English), *SF Bay Area Review*, No 25 1982

'Radar and Gyroscope', *A+U*, April 1982

'About Diversity', (English), *JA*, October 1983

'On Henning Larsen', *A+U*, January 1983

'On Van Nelle Factory', *A+U*, October 1983

'Koten and Klassik', (English), *Architectural Design*, 7/8 1984

'Duality of Style', (English), *JA*, June 1984

'Recent Work', (English), *JA*, September 1984

'Tokyo Urban Language', (editor), *Process Architecture*, No 49 August 1984

'Architectural Education in America', (English), *JA*, October 1986; *Shinkenchiku*, September 1986

'Formality and Informality', *JA*, September 1987

'An Oxymoronic Approach to Architecture', (English), *JA*, January 1987

'*Parole* of Architecture and Colour', *Musashino Art*, Vol 73 1988

'Relativism in Architecture', *Shinkenchiku*, August 1991

'Talking Takeyamese', (interview in English), *Reflections* (University of Illinois Urbana-Champaign), No 8 1991

'Imagination in Architecture', *Japanese Institute of Architects Report*, the Shizuoka Chapter, October 1992

'Trans-culturalism in Architecture', *Architect, JIA*, November 1992

'Work Analysis', *Kenchiku Zasshi* (AIJ Journal), January 1993

'Port Terminal – Architecture of the Year', *Kenchiku Zasshi* (AIJ Journal), March 1993

Publications by Minoru Takeyama

Books only

Blue Nirvana; Language versus Architecture, Image Press; and Shoten Kenchiku-sha (Tokyo) 1973

Meaning of Streets, Kajima Shuppan-sha (Tokyo) 1977

Architects' Drawings: Minoru Takeyama, Graphic-sha (Tokyo) 1982

Language in Architecture, Kajima Shuppan-sha, (Tokyo) 1984

Publications by Minoru Takeyama

Chapters to books

'Jorn Utzon and His Intention', in Kojiro, Yuichiro (ed),*Contemporary Form Givers,* Kajima Shuppan-sha (Tokyo) 1966

'Architecture and Music', *World Music*, Kawade Shuppan-sha (Tokyo) 1969

'Space Perception', Noboru Kawazoe (ed), *Scope of Design,* Fudo-sha (Tokyo) 1969

'Interior Design', *Yearbook of Interior Design Association* (Tokyo) 1971

'My Intentions', *Autobiography of Japanese Architects,* Series No 24, Sanichi Shobo (Tokyo) 1973

'Heterology in Architecture', Frampton, Kenneth (ed), *A New Wave of Japanese Architecture – Catalogue 10,* Institute of Architecture and Urban Studies (New York) 1978

'Architectural Rhetoric', *Design Year Book,* Kodansha (Tokyo) 1984

'Recognition Map', *Meeting with Architecture,* Shokoku-sha (Tokyo) 1988

'Living Space as a Sign', *Interior Semiotics = Space Adventure No 3,* INAX (Tokyo) 1992

'Landscape Architecture in America', *Ground Design,* Sogo Uni-Com (Tokyo) 1992

Publications by Minoru Takeyama

Translations by Takeyama

Jencks, Charles, *The Language of Post-Modern Architecture,* (Academy Editions, London), translation, A+U (Tokyo) 1978

Publications on Minoru Takeyama

Books only

Jencks, Charles, *Modern Movements in Architecture,* Penguin Books (London); Doubleday Anchor Books (New York) 1973

—, *A Guide to Japanese Architecture,* Shinkenchiku-sha (Tokyo) 1975

—, *The Language of Post Modern Architecture,* Academy Editions (London) 1977

Ross, Michael Franklin, *Beyond Metabolism; New Japanese Architecture,* Architectural Record Books; McGraw Hill (New York) 1978

Frampton, Kenneth (ed), *A New Wave of Japanese Architecture – Catalogue 10,* IAUS (New York) 1978

Bognar, Botond, *Mai Japan Epiteszet,* (Hungarian), Muszaki Konyvkiado (Budapest) 1979

Fawcett, Chris, *The New Japanese House,* Harper and Row (New York) 1980

Porter, Tom, *Color Outside,* Architecture Press (London) 1981

—, *Contemporary Architects,* MacMillan (London) 1982

Dom, Nas, *50 Outstanding Architects,* (Yugoslavia) 1983

—, *GA Houses 14: Japanese Houses,* ADA Edita (Tokyo) 1983

Wurman, Richard Saul, *Tokyo Access,* Access Press (Los Angeles); and C Itoh (Tokyo) 1984

Suzuki, Hiroyuki, Reyner Banham and Katsuhiro Kobayashi, *Contemporary Architecture of Japan; 1958-84,* Rizzoli (New York) 1985

Bognar, Botond, *Contemporary Japanese Architecture,* Van Nostrand Reinhold (New York) 1985

Popham, Peter, *Tokyo: the City at the End of the World*, Kodansha International (Tokyo) 1986

—, *Vision der Moderne – Das Princip Konstruktion*, DAM (Deutsches Architekturmuseum) (West Germany) 1986

Bognar, Botond, *The New Japanese Architecture*, Rizzoli (New York) 1990

Bognar, Botond (ed), *Japanese Architecture II, AD Profile 99*, Academy Editions (London) 1990

Mladjenovic, Ivica, *Belgrade Triennal of World Architecture*, Union of Architects of Serbia (Belgrade) 1992

Kurokawa, Kisho, *New Wave Japanese Architecture*, Academy Editions (London) 1993

—, *Kenchiku Guide Book 1864–1993*, Shinkenchiku-sha (Tokyo) 1994

—, Architectural Map of Tokyo, Gallery MA; and Toto Shuppan-sha (Tokyo) 1994

Bognar, Botond, *The Japan Guide*, Princeton Architectural Press (New York) 1995

Periodicals

The works in this issue

Labour Union Hall, Fuji Heavy Industries

Shinkenchiku, Japan; *Kenchiku Bunka* – June 1970; *Space Design*, Japan – August 1970; *Progressive Architecture*, USA – September 1971; *Architectural Design*, UK– July 1971; *Arkitektur* – February 1972; *AA* – January 1972

Ichiban-kan + Niban-kan

Shinkenchiku, Japan; *Shoten Kenchiku*, Japan; *Japan Interior*; *KK* – April 1970 + July 1970; *Space Design*, Japan; *Kenchiku*, Japan; *Detail* – July 1970; *JA* – August 1970; *Architectural Design*, UK – September 1970; *Domus* – October 1970; *Mobilia* – December 1970

Iwakura Office

Shinkenchiku, Japan; *Japan Interior* – March 1972; *JA* – July 1972

Pepsi-Cola Bottling Plant

Kenchiku, Japan – January 1973; *Shinkenchiku*, Japan; *Kenchiku Bunka*; *Japan Interior* – August 1973; *JA* – November 1973; *Design* – February 1974; *Progressive Architecture*, USA – March 1974; *B+W* – May 1974

Hotel Beverly Tom

Shinkenchiku, Japan; *Space Design*, Japan; *Kenchiku Bunka*; *Japan Interior* – January 1974; *JA* – April 1974; *Detail* – Spring 1974

Shu-Pub

Shoten Kenchiku, Japan – January 1970; *Detail* – July 1970

Iwakura Residence

Shinkenchiku, Japan; *Kenchiku Bunka*; *Japan Interior* – August 1974; *JA* – November/December 1974; *SA* – September 1974

Atelier Indigo

Shinkenchiku, Japan; *Kenchiku Bunka*; *Japan Interior*; *Design*; *Kenchiku Gaho* – September 1977

Nakamura Memorial Hospital

Japan Interior – January 1981; *Shinkenchiku*, Japan; *Kenchiku Bunka*; *Japan Interior*; *Nikkei Architecture* – July 1981; *Architectural Design*, UK – January/February 1982; *Process Architecture* No 42 – 1983; *Contemporary Architecture* Vol 4 – 1983

Building No. 10, Musashino

Shinkenchiku, Japan; *Kenchiku Bunka* – April 1982; *JA* – August 1982; *Progressive Architecture*, USA – December 1982; *Contemporary Architecture* Vol 5 – 1984

Mikakuto Factory

Shinkenchiku, Japan; *Kenchiku Bunka* – August 1985; *JA* – September 1985; *Baumeister* – June 1986; *Progressive Architecture* – October 1987

Renaissance, Kyoto

Shinkenchiku, Japan; *Shoten Kenchiku*, Japan – August 1986; *NA*, Japan – July 28, 1986; *ICON* – September 1986; *JA* – January 1987

Egyptian Embassy, Tokyo

Shinkenchiku, Japan; *Kenchiku Bunka* – June 1987; *NA*, Japan – June 1, 1987; *JA* – July 1987

Tokyo Port Terminal

Shinkenchiku, Japan – August 1991; *JA* – August 1991; *NA*, Japan – August 1991; *Shoten Kenchiku*, Japan – August 1991; *Seko* – February 1992; *Architectural Design*, UK – November 1992